Slow Cooker
WINNING RECIPES

Publications International, Ltd.

Some of the products listed in this publication may be in limited distribution.

Pictured on the front cover *(left to right):* Chunky Pinto Bean Dip *(page 10),* Cheesy Corn and Peppers *(page 106),* Easy Dirty Rice *(page 110),* Southwestern Corn and Beans *(page 118),* Potato Cheddar Soup *(page 44),* Fiesta Black Bean Soup *(page 28),* My Mother's Sausage & Vegetable Soup *(page 36)* and Chunky Ranch Potatoes *(page 116).*
Pictured on the back cover *(top to bottom):* Mini Swiss Steak Sandwiches *(page 22)* and Coq au Vin *(page 57).*

ISBN-13: 978-1-4127-9793-1
ISBN-10: 1-4127-9793-4

Library of Congress Control Number: 2009920600

Manufactured in China.

8 7 6 5 4 3 2 1

Microwave Cooking: Microwave ovens vary in wattage. Use the cooking times as guidelines and check for doneness before adding more time.

Preparation/Cooking Times: Preparation times are based on the approximate amount of time required to assemble the recipe before cooking, baking, chilling or serving. These times include preparation steps such as measuring, chopping and mixing. The fact that some preparations and cooking can be done simultaneously is taken into account. Preparation of optional ingredients and serving suggestions is not included.

Table of Contents

Satisfying Small Bites

Sweet and Spicy Sausage Rounds

  1 pound kielbasa sausage, cut into ¼-inch-thick rounds
  ⅔ cup blackberry jam
  ⅓ cup steak sauce
  1 tablespoon prepared yellow mustard
  ½ teaspoon ground allspice

1. Place all ingredients in slow cooker; toss to coat completely. Cover; cook on HIGH 3 hours or until richly glazed.

2. Serve with decorative cocktail picks.   *Makes 3 cups*

Editor's Note

Yum! The salty-sweet flavor combination in this appetizer is not to be missed. You may want to double this recipe, because these sausage rounds will be gone before you know it!

Apricot and Brie Dip

½ cup dried apricots, finely chopped
⅓ cup plus 1 tablespoon apricot preserves, divided
¼ cup apple juice
1 (2-pound) Brie, rind removed, cut into cubes
Bread slices, crackers or crudités for dipping

1. Combine dried apricots, ⅓ cup apricot preserves and apple juice in 3½- to 4-quart slow cooker. Cover; cook on HIGH 40 minutes.

2. Stir in Brie. Cover; cook 30 to 40 minutes longer or until melted. Stir in remaining 1 tablespoon preserves. Turn slow cooker to low and serve with bread slices, crackers or crudités.

Makes 8 to 12 servings

Prep Time: 10 minutes • **Cook Time:** 1 hour 10 minutes to 1 hour 20 minutes

Kitchen Tip

Look for a round of Brie that is no more than 1 inch thick. If it's too thick, the cheese can become overripe along the edge before fully ripening in the center.

Apricot and Brie Dip

Slow-Cooked Mini Pulled Pork Bites

1 can (10¾ ounces) CAMPBELL'S® Condensed Tomato Soup
½ cup packed brown sugar
¼ cup cider vinegar
1 teaspoon garlic powder
4 pounds boneless pork shoulder
1 package (13.9 ounces) PEPPERIDGE FARM® Soft Country Style Dinner Rolls
Hot pepper sauce (optional)

1. Stir the soup, brown sugar, vinegar and garlic powder in a 6-quart slow cooker. Add the pork and turn to coat.

2. Cover and cook on LOW for 6 to 7 hours* or until the pork is fork-tender.

3. Remove the pork from the cooker to a cutting board and let stand for 10 minutes. Using 2 forks, shred the pork. Return the pork to the cooker.

4. Divide the pork mixture among the rolls. Serve with the hot pepper sauce, if desired.   *Makes 16 mini sandwiches*

Or on HIGH for 4 to 5 hours.

Prep Time: 10 minutes • **Cook Time:** 6 to 7 hours •
Stand Time: 10 minutes

 *Kitchen Tip*

Boneless pork shoulder is also referred to as pork butt. This inexpensive cut of meat becomes juicy and tender when cooked in the slow cooker.

Slow-Cooked Mini Pulled Pork Bites

Chunky Pinto Bean Dip

2 cans (15 ounces each) pinto beans, rinsed and drained
1 can (about 14 ounces) diced tomatoes with mild green chiles
1 cup chopped onion
⅔ cup chunky salsa
1 tablespoon vegetable oil
1½ teaspoons minced garlic
1 teaspoon ground coriander
1 teaspoon ground cumin
1½ cups (6 ounces) shredded Mexican cheese blend or Cheddar cheese
¼ cup chopped fresh cilantro
Blue corn or other tortilla chips
Assorted raw vegetables

1. Combine beans, tomatoes, onion, salsa, oil, garlic, coriander and cumin in slow cooker.

2. Cover; cook on LOW 5 to 6 hours or until onion is tender.

3. Partially mash bean mixture with potato masher. Stir in cheese and cilantro. Serve at room temperature with chips and vegetables.

Makes about 5 cups dip

Prep Time: 12 minutes • **Cook Time:** 5 to 6 hours

Editor's Note

This bean dip is sure to become a staple at parties. The earthy flavors of the southwest and the creamy texture of the pinto beans will keep you dipping until there's nothing left.

Chunky Pinto Bean Dip

Sausage and Swiss Chard Stuffed Mushrooms

2 packages (6 ounces each) baby portobello mushrooms or large
   brown stuffing mushrooms*
4 tablespoons extra-virgin olive oil, divided
½ teaspoon salt, divided
½ teaspoon black pepper, divided
½ pound bulk pork sausage
½ onion, finely chopped
2 cups chopped Swiss chard, rinsed
¼ teaspoon dried thyme
2 tablespoons garlic-and-herb-flavored dried bread crumbs
1½ cups chicken broth, divided
2 tablespoons grated Parmesan cheese
2 tablespoons chopped fresh parsley

*Use "baby bellas" or cremini mushrooms. Do not substitute white button mushrooms.

1. Coat 5- to 6-quart slow cooker with nonstick cooking spray.
Wipe mushrooms clean, remove stems and hollow out caps. Pour
3 tablespoons oil into small bowl. Brush mushrooms with oil; season
with ¼ teaspoon salt and ¼ teaspoon pepper; set aside.

2. Heat remaining 1 tablespoon oil in medium skillet over medium
heat; add sausage. Cook and stir until browned. Drain sausage on
paper towel.

3. Add onion to skillet; cook and stir, loosening browned bits, about
3 minutes or until translucent. Stir in Swiss chard and thyme. Cook
1 to 2 minutes or until Swiss chard is just wilted. Remove skillet from
heat.

4. Add sausage, bread crumbs, 1 tablespoon broth, remaining
¼ teaspoon salt and ¼ teaspoon pepper to skillet; mix well. Scoop
1 tablespoon of stuffing into each mushroom cap.

5. Pour remaining broth into slow cooker. Arrange stuffed mushrooms in bottom. Cover; cook on HIGH 3 hours or until mushrooms are tender. To serve, remove mushrooms with slotted spoon; discard cooking liquid. Sprinkle with cheese and parsley.

Makes 6 to 8 servings

Prep Time: 20 minutes • **Cook Time:** 3 hours

Mahogany Wings

1 can (10½ ounces) CAMPBELL'S® Condensed Beef Broth
2 bunches green onions, chopped
1 cup soy sauce
1 cup plum sauce
6 cloves garlic, minced
½ cup light molasses or honey
¼ cup cider vinegar
6 pounds chicken wings
1 tablespoon cornstarch

1. Stir the broth, onions, soy sauce, plum sauce, garlic, molasses and vinegar in a 6-quart slow cooker removable insert.*

2. Cut off the chicken wing tips and discard. Cut the chicken wings in half at the joint. Add the chicken to the cooker and stir to coat. Cover and refrigerate for 6 hours or overnight.

3. Stir ½ **cup** of the marinade and cornstarch in a small bowl. Stir into the chicken mixture.

4. Cover and cook on HIGH for 4 to 5 hours** or until the chicken is cooked through.

Makes 18 servings

If your slow cooker doesn't have a removable insert, you can stir the marinade ingredients into a large bowl instead. Add the chicken and stir to coat. Cover and refrigerate as directed. Pour the chicken mixture into the cooker and proceed with Steps 3 and 4 as directed.

**Or on LOW for 7 to 8 hours.*

Prep Time: 30 minutes • **Marinate Time:** 6 hours •
Cook Time: 4 to 5 hours

Chili con Queso

1 package (16 ounces) pasteurized process cheese, cubed
1 can (10 ounces) diced tomatoes with green chiles
1 cup sliced green onions
2 teaspoons ground coriander
2 teaspoons ground cumin
¾ teaspoon hot pepper sauce
  Green onion strips (optional)
  Jalapeño pepper slices (optional)
  Tortilla chips

1. Combine cheese, tomatoes, green onions, coriander, cumin and hot pepper sauce in 1½-quart slow cooker; stir until well blended.

2. Cover; cook on LOW 2 to 3 hours or until heated through.

3. Garnish with green onion strips and jalapeño slices, if desired. Serve with tortilla chips.   *Makes 3 cups*

Serving Suggestion: For something different, serve this dip with pita chips.

Curried Snack Mix

3 tablespoons butter
2 tablespoons packed light brown sugar
1½ teaspoons hot curry powder
¼ teaspoon salt
¼ teaspoon ground cumin
2 cups rice cereal squares
1 cup walnut halves
1 cup dried cranberries

Melt butter in large skillet. Add brown sugar, curry powder, salt and cumin; mix well. Add cereal, walnuts and cranberries; stir to coat. Transfer mixture to slow cooker. Cover; cook on LOW 3 hours. Cook, uncovered, 30 minutes.   *Makes 16 servings*

Chili con Queso

Shrimp Fondue Dip

1 pound medium raw shrimp, peeled and deveined
½ cup water
½ teaspoon salt, divided
2 tablespoons butter
4 teaspoons Dijon mustard
6 slices thick-sliced white bread, crusts removed
2 eggs, beaten
1 cup milk
¼ teaspoon black pepper
2 cups (8 ounces) shredded Gruyère or Swiss cheese
   Crusty French bread, sliced

1. Coat slow cooker with nonstick cooking spray. Place shrimp, water and ¼ teaspoon salt in small saucepan. Cover; cook over medium heat about 3 minutes or until shrimp are pink and opaque. Remove shrimp with slotted spoon; reserve ½ cup broth.

2. Combine butter and mustard in small bowl. Spread mixture onto bread slices. Cut bread into 1-inch cubes.

3. Beat eggs, milk, reserved ½ cup broth, remaining ¼ teaspoon salt and pepper in small bowl.

4. Spread ⅓ of bread cubes in bottom of slow cooker. Top with ⅓ of shrimp. Sprinkle with ⅓ of cheese. Repeat layers 2 more times. Pour egg mixture over layers. Use rubber spatula to push bread below surface to absorb liquid. Line lid with 2 paper towels. Cover; cook on LOW 2 hours or until mixture is hot and thick. Serve with French bread for dipping. *Makes about 5 cups*

Prep Time: 15 minutes • **Cook Time:** 2 hours

Shrimp Fondue Dip

Barbecued Meatballs

2 pounds ground beef
1⅓ cups ketchup, divided
3 tablespoons seasoned dry bread crumbs
1 egg, lightly beaten
2 tablespoons dried onion flakes
¾ teaspoon garlic salt
½ teaspoon black pepper
1 cup packed light brown sugar
1 can (6 ounces) tomato paste
¼ cup soy sauce
¼ cup cider vinegar
1½ teaspoons hot pepper sauce
Diced bell peppers (optional)

1. Preheat oven to 350°F. Combine ground beef, ⅓ cup ketchup, bread crumbs, egg, onion flakes, garlic salt and black pepper in medium bowl. Mix lightly but thoroughly; shape into 1-inch meatballs.

2. Place meatballs on two 15×10-inch jelly-roll pans or shallow roasting pans. Bake 18 minutes or until browned. Transfer meatballs to slow cooker.

3. Mix remaining 1 cup ketchup, brown sugar, tomato paste, soy sauce, vinegar and hot pepper sauce in medium bowl. Pour over meatballs. Cover; cook on LOW 4 hours. Garnish with bell peppers, if desired. Serve with cocktail picks.

Makes about 4 dozen meatballs

Barbecued Franks: Arrange 2 (12-ounce) packages or 3 (8-ounce) packages cocktail franks in slow cooker. Combine 1 cup ketchup with brown sugar, tomato paste, soy sauce, vinegar and hot pepper sauce in medium bowl; pour over franks. Cover; cook on LOW 4 hours.

Barbecued Meatballs

Artichoke and Nacho Cheese Dip

2 cans (10¾ ounces each) condensed nacho cheese soup, undiluted
1 can (14 ounces) quartered artichoke hearts, drained and coarsely chopped
1 cup (4 ounces) shredded or thinly sliced pepper jack cheese
1 can (4 ounces) evaporated milk
2 tablespoons minced chives, divided
½ teaspoon paprika
Crackers or chips

1. Combine soup, artichoke hearts, cheese, evaporated milk, 1 tablespoon chives and paprika in slow cooker. Cover; cook on LOW 2 hours.

2. Stir well. Sprinkle with remaining 1 tablespoon chives and serve with crackers.   *Makes about 1 quart*

Prep Time: 5 minutes • **Cook Time:** 2 hours

Editor's Note

The simplicity of this tasty dip makes it a winner! By using mostly pantry goods, you can always keep the ingredients on hand for a quick and satisfying starter.

Artichoke and Nacho Cheese Dip

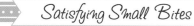

Mini Swiss Steak Sandwiches

  2 tablespoons all-purpose flour
  ¼ teaspoon salt
  ¼ teaspoon black pepper
1¾ pounds boneless beef chuck steak, about 1 inch thick
  2 tablespoons vegetable oil
  1 medium onion, sliced
  1 green bell pepper, cored, seeded and sliced into strips
  1 clove garlic, sliced
  1 cup stewed tomatoes
  ¾ cup condensed beef consommé, undiluted
  2 teaspoons Worcestershire sauce
  1 bay leaf
  2 tablespoons cornstarch
  2 packages (12 ounces each) sweet Hawaiian-style dinner rolls,
     split into halves

1. Coat slow cooker with nonstick cooking spray. Combine flour, salt and black pepper in large resealable food storage bag. Add steak and shake well to coat.

2. Heat oil in large skillet over high heat. Brown steak on both sides. Transfer to slow cooker.

3. Add onion and bell pepper to skillet; cook and stir over medium-high heat 3 to 4 minutes or until softened. Add garlic; cook and stir 30 seconds. Pour mixture over steak.

4. Add tomatoes, consommé, Worcestershire sauce and bay leaf to slow cooker. Cover; cook on HIGH 3½ hours or until steak is tender. Transfer steak to cutting board. Remove and discard bay leaf.

5. Blend cornstarch with 2 tablespoons cooking liquid in small bowl until smooth. Stir into cooking liquid in slow cooker; cook 10 minutes or until thickened.

6. Meanwhile, thinly slice steak against the grain. Return to slow cooker. Add salt and pepper; mix well to combine. Serve steak mixture on warm rolls.   *Makes 16 to 18 sandwiches*

Prep Time: 15 minutes • **Cook Time:** 3¾ hours

Mini Swiss Steak Sandwiches

Steaming Soups & Stews

Pasta Fagioli Soup

2 cans (about 14 ounces each) beef or vegetable broth
1 can (about 15 ounces) Great Northern beans, rinsed and drained
1 can (about 14 ounces) diced tomatoes
2 medium zucchini, quartered lengthwise and sliced
1 tablespoon olive oil
1½ teaspoons minced garlic
½ teaspoon dried basil
½ teaspoon dried oregano
½ cup uncooked tubetti, ditali or small shell pasta
½ cup garlic seasoned croutons
½ cup grated Asiago or Romano cheese
3 tablespoons chopped fresh basil or Italian parsley (optional)

1. Combine broth, beans, tomatoes, zucchini, oil, garlic, dried basil and oregano in slow cooker; mix well. Cover; cook on LOW 3 to 4 hours.

2. Stir in pasta. Cover; cook on LOW 1 hour or until pasta is tender.

3. Serve soup with croutons and cheese. Garnish with fresh basil.

Makes 5 to 6 servings

Prep Time: 12 minutes • **Cook Time:** 4 to 5 hours

Caribbean Sweet Potato & Bean Stew

2 medium sweet potatoes (about 1 pound), peeled and cut into
    1-inch cubes
2 cups frozen cut green beans
1 can (about 15 ounces) black beans, rinsed and drained
1 can (about 14 ounces) vegetable broth
1 small onion, sliced
2 teaspoons Caribbean jerk seasoning
½ teaspoon dried thyme
¼ teaspoon salt
¼ teaspoon ground cinnamon
⅓ cup slivered almonds, toasted*
    Hot pepper sauce (optional)

To toast almonds, spread in single layer on baking sheet. Bake in preheated 350°F oven 8 to 10 minutes or until golden brown, stirring frequently.

1. Combine sweet potatoes, beans, broth, onion, jerk seasoning, thyme, salt and cinnamon in slow cooker. Cover; cook on LOW 5 to 6 hours or until vegetables are tender.

2. Serve with almonds and hot pepper sauce, if desired.

Makes 4 servings

Prep Time: 10 minutes • **Cook Time:** 5 to 6 hours

Hearty Beef & Bean Chili

½ pound boneless chuck roast, cut into large chunks
1 can (28 ounces) HUNT'S® Whole Tomatoes
1 can (6 ounces) HUNT'S® Tomato Paste
1 can (30 ounces) HUNT'S® Chili Beans
1 packet (1¼ ounces) chili seasoning mix

1. Combine roast, tomatoes, tomato paste, beans and seasoning mix in slow cooker.

2. Cover and cook on LOW for 8 to 10 hours or on HIGH for 4 to 6 hours.

Makes 8 servings

Prep Time: 5 minutes • **Cook Time:** 8 to 10 hours (LOW) or 4 to 6 hours (HIGH)

Caribbean Sweet Potato & Bean Stew

Fiesta Black Bean Soup

6 cups chicken broth
12 ounces potatoes, peeled and diced
1 can (about 15 ounces) black beans, rinsed and drained
½ pound cooked ham, diced
½ onion, diced
1 can (4 ounces) chopped jalapeño peppers
2 cloves garlic, minced
2 teaspoons dried oregano
1½ teaspoons dried thyme
1 teaspoon ground cumin
  Toppings: sour cream, chopped bell pepper and chopped tomatoes

1. Combine broth, potatoes, beans, ham, onion, jalapeño peppers, garlic, oregano, thyme and cumin in slow cooker; mix well.

2. Cover; cook on LOW 8 to 10 hours or on HIGH 4 to 5 hours.

3. Adjust seasonings. Serve with desired toppings.

Makes 6 to 8 servings

Easy Beef Stew

1½ to 2 pounds beef stew meat
4 medium potatoes, cubed
4 carrots, cut into 1½-inch pieces *or* 4 cups baby carrots
1 medium onion, cut into 8 pieces
2 cans (8 ounces each) tomato sauce
1 teaspoon salt
½ teaspoon black pepper

Combine all ingredients in slow cooker. Cover; cook on LOW 8 to 10 hours or until vegetables are tender.   *Makes 6 to 8 servings*

Fiesta Black Bean Soup

New Mexican Green Chile Pork Stew

1½ pounds boneless pork shoulder, cut into 1-inch cubes
2 medium baking potatoes or sweet potatoes, peeled and cut into large chunks
1 cup chopped onion
1 can (4 ounces) diced green chiles
1 cup frozen corn
2 teaspoons sugar
2 teaspoons cumin or chili powder
1 teaspoon dried oregano
1 jar (16 ounces) salsa verde (green salsa)
Hot cooked rice
¼ cup chopped fresh cilantro

1. Place pork, potatoes, onion, chiles and corn into 4-quart slow cooker. Stir sugar, cumin and oregano into salsa and pour over pork and vegetables. Stir gently to mix.

2. Cover; cook on LOW 6 to 8 hours or on HIGH 4 to 5 hours until pork is tender. Serve stew over hot rice and garnish with cilantro.

Makes 6 servings

Prep Time: 15 minutes • **Cook Time:** 6 to 8 hours (LOW) or 4 to 5 hours (HIGH)

Editor's Note

This hearty stew is perfect for a weeknight meal or special occasion. The fragrant and tender pork will melt in your mouth.

New Mexican Green Chile Pork Stew

Classic French Onion Soup

¼ cup (½ stick) butter
3 large yellow onions, sliced
1 cup dry white wine
3 cans (about 14 ounces each) beef or chicken broth
1 teaspoon Worcestershire sauce
½ teaspoon salt
½ teaspoon dried thyme
4 slices French bread, toasted
1 cup (4 ounces) shredded Swiss cheese

1. Melt butter in large skillet over medium heat. Add onions; cook and stir 15 minutes or until onions are soft and lightly browned. Stir in wine.

2. Combine onion mixture, broth, Worcestershire sauce, salt and thyme in slow cooker. Cover; cook on LOW 4 to 4½ hours.

3. Preheat broiler. Ladle soup into 4 bowls; top with bread slice and cheese. Broil soups 2 minutes or until cheese is melted.

Makes 4 servings

Chorizo Chili

1 pound ground beef
8 ounces bulk raw chorizo
1 can (about 16 ounces) chili beans in chili sauce
2 cans (about 14 ounces each) zesty chili-style diced tomatoes

1. Place beef and chorizo in slow cooker. Stir to break up well.

2. Stir in beans and tomatoes. Cover; cook on LOW 7 hours. Skim off and discard excess fat before serving. *Makes 6 servings*

Serving Suggestion: Top with sour cream or shredded cheese.

Prep Time: 5 minutes • **Cook Time:** 7 hours

Classic French Onion Soup

Italian Hillside Garden Soup

1 tablespoon olive oil
1 cup chopped onion
1 cup chopped green bell pepper
½ cup sliced celery
2 cans (about 14 ounces each) chicken broth
1 can (about 14 ounces) diced tomatoes with basil, garlic and oregano
1 can (about 15 ounces) navy beans, rinsed and drained
1 medium zucchini, chopped
1 cup frozen cut green beans, thawed
¼ teaspoon garlic powder
1 package (9 ounces) refrigerated sausage- or cheese-filled tortellini pasta
3 tablespoons chopped fresh basil
Grated Asiago or Parmesan cheese (optional)

1. Heat oil in large skillet over medium-high heat. Add onion, bell pepper and celery; cook and stir 4 minutes or until onions are translucent. Transfer to 5-quart slow cooker.

2. Add broth, tomatoes, navy beans, zucchini, green beans and garlic powder. Cover; cook on LOW 7 hours or on HIGH 3½ hours.

3. Turn slow cooker to HIGH. Add tortellini and cook 20 to 25 minutes or until pasta is tender. Stir in basil. Garnish with cheese.

Makes 6 servings

Prep Time: 15 minutes • **Cook Time:** 7 hours (LOW) or 3½ hours (HIGH), plus 20 minutes (HIGH)

Kitchen Tip

Freeze leftover soup in individual containers for a perfect grab-and-go lunch. Just thaw and then reheat in the microwave.

Lamb Shank and Mushroom Stew

2 tablespoons olive oil, divided
2 large lamb shanks (about 2 pounds)
2 tablespoons all-purpose flour
2 cups sliced mushrooms
1 small red onion, thinly sliced
1 garlic clove, minced
1¼ cups chicken broth
½ cup pitted sliced green olives
¼ teaspoon salt, or to taste
⅛ teaspoon black pepper, or to taste
⅛ teaspoon dried thyme
2 tablespoons capers
4 cups cooked noodles

1. Heat 1 tablespoon oil in large skillet over medium-high heat. Dust lamb shanks with flour, reserving leftover flour. Brown lamb on all sides, about 3 minutes per side. Transfer to 5- or 6-quart slow cooker.

2. Heat remaining tablespoon oil in skillet; add mushrooms, onion and garlic. Cook and stir 3 minutes or until vegetables are tender. Transfer mixture to slow cooker.

3. Sprinkle reserved flour into skillet and stir. Pour chicken broth into skillet. Stir to scrape up any browned bits; continue to cook and stir 2 minutes or until mixture is slightly thickened. Pour into slow cooker.

4. Stir in olives, salt, pepper and thyme. Cover; cook on LOW 7 to 8 hours or on HIGH 4 to 5 hours.

5. Transfer lamb to cutting board. Gently pull lamb meat from bones with fork. Discard bones. Let cooking liquid stand 5 minutes. Skim off and discard excess fat. Return lamb to slow cooker. Stir in capers. Adjust seasoning, if desired. Serve lamb and sauce over noodles.

Makes 4 servings

Prep Time: 20 minutes • **Cook Time:** 7 to 8 hours (LOW) or 4 to 5 hours (HIGH)

My Mother's Sausage & Vegetable Soup

2 cups diced potatoes
1 can (about 15 ounces) black beans, rinsed and drained
1 can (about 14 ounces) diced tomatoes
1 can (10¾ ounces) condensed cream of mushroom soup, undiluted
½ pound turkey sausage, cut into ½-inch slices
1 cup chopped onion
1 cup chopped red bell pepper
½ cup water
2 teaspoons prepared horseradish
2 teaspoons honey
1 teaspoon dried basil

Combine all ingredients in slow cooker, mix well. Cover; cook on LOW 7 to 8 hours or until potatoes are tender.   *Makes 6 to 8 servings*

Lentil Soup with Beef

3 cans (10½ ounces **each**) CAMPBELL'S® Condensed French Onion Soup
1 soup can water
3 stalks celery, sliced (about 1½ cups)
3 large carrots, sliced (about 1½ cups)
1½ cups dried lentils
1 can (about 14.5 ounces) diced tomatoes
1 teaspoon dried thyme leaves, crushed
3 cloves garlic, minced
2 pounds beef for stew, cut into 1-inch pieces

1. Stir the soup, water, celery, carrots, lentils, tomatoes, thyme, garlic and beef in a 5-quart slow cooker. Season as desired.

2. Cover and cook on LOW for 7 to 8 hours* or until the beef is fork-tender.   *Makes 8 servings*

Or on HIGH for 4 to 5 hours.

Prep Time: 15 minutes • **Cook Time:** 7 hours

My Mother's Sausage & Vegetable Soup

Jambalaya

2½ to 3 pounds chicken pieces, skinned if desired
1 can (14½ ounces) diced tomatoes
1 can (14½ ounces) chicken broth
1 green bell pepper, chopped
2 cups *French's*® French Fried Onions
¼ cup *Frank's*® *RedHot*® Cayenne Pepper Sauce
2 cloves garlic, chopped
2 teaspoons Old Bay ® seafood seasoning
1½ teaspoons dried oregano leaves
¾ teaspoon salt
½ teaspoon ground black pepper
1 cup uncooked regular rice
1 pound medium raw shrimp, peeled and deveined

1. Combine the chicken, tomatoes, chicken broth, green pepper, 1 cup *French's*® French Fried Onions, *Frank's*® *RedHot*® Cayenne Pepper Sauce, garlic, seafood seasoning, oregano, salt and pepper in the slow cooker. Cover and cook on LOW for 4 to 5 hours or on HIGH for 2 to 2½ hours.

2. Stir in the rice. Cook on LOW for 2 hours or on HIGH for 1 hour or until rice is cooked and all liquid is absorbed.

3. Turn slow cooker to HIGH. Add shrimp. Cover and cook 30 minutes or until shrimp are pink. Arrange jambalaya on serving platter. Sprinkle with remaining French Fried Onions.   *Makes 6 servings*

Editor's Note

This Creole specialty will warm you from the inside out, making Jambalaya a true soul food.

Jambalaya

Sweet Potato Stew

1 cup *each* chopped onion and celery
1 cup grated peeled sweet potato
1 cup vegetable broth or water
2 slices bacon, crisp-cooked and crumbled, plus additional for garnish
1 cup half-and-half
   Black pepper
¼ cup minced fresh parsley

1. Place onion, celery, sweet potato, broth and bacon in slow cooker. Cover; cook on LOW 6 hours or until vegetables are tender.

2. Turn slow cooker to HIGH. Add half-and-half to reach desired consistency. Add water, if needed. Cook, uncovered, 30 minutes on HIGH or until heated through. Season to taste with pepper. Sprinkle with bacon and parsley. *Makes 4 servings*

White Bean with Fennel Soup

4 cups SWANSON® Vegetable Broth (Regular **or** Certified Organic)
⅛ teaspoon ground black pepper
1 small bulb fennel (about ½ pound), trimmed and sliced (about 2 cups)
1 small onion, chopped (about ½ cup)
2 cloves garlic, minced
1 package (10 ounces) frozen leaf spinach
1 can (14½ ounces) diced tomatoes
1 can (about 16 ounces) white kidney (cannellini) beans, undrained

1. Stir the broth, black pepper, fennel, onion and garlic in a 5½- or 6-quart slow cooker.

2. Cover and cook on LOW for 6 to 7 hours.

3. Add the spinach, tomatoes and beans. Turn the heat to HIGH. Cover and cook for 1 hour more or until the vegetables are tender.

Makes 6 servings

Sweet Potato Stew

Lamb and Vegetable Stew

2 cups sliced mushrooms
1 large red bell pepper, diced
1 large carrot, cut into ½-inch-thick slices
1 small unpeeled new potato, diced
1 small parsnip, cut into ½-inch-thick slices
1 large leek, chopped
½ cup chicken broth
1 clove garlic, minced
½ teaspoon dried thyme
¼ teaspoon dried rosemary
⅛ teaspoon black pepper
12 ounces lamb shoulder meat, cut into 1-inch pieces
2 tablespoons all-purpose flour
½ teaspoon salt (optional)

1. Combine mushrooms, bell pepper, carrot, potato, parsnip, leek, broth, garlic, thyme, rosemary and black pepper in slow cooker. Add lamb. Cover; cook on LOW 6 to 7 hours.

2. Combine flour, 2 tablespoons liquid from slow cooker and salt in small bowl. Stir flour mixture into slow cooker. Cover; cook 10 minutes.

Makes 4 servings

Kitchen Tip

Lamb is meat from a sheep less than 1 year old. The younger the animal, the more tender the meat will be.

Lamb and Vegetable Stew

Potato Cheddar Soup

2 pounds new red potatoes, peeled and cut into ½-inch cubes
¾ cup coarsely chopped carrots
1 medium onion, coarsely chopped
3 cups chicken broth
½ teaspoon salt
1 cup half-and-half
¼ teaspoon black pepper
2 cups (8 ounces) shredded Cheddar cheese

1. Place potatoes, carrots, onion, broth and salt in slow cooker. Cover; cook on LOW 6 to 7 hours or on HIGH 3 to 3½ hours or until vegetables are tender.

2. Stir in half-and-half and pepper. Cover; cook on HIGH 15 minutes. Turn off heat and remove cover; let stand 5 minutes. Stir in cheese until melted. *Makes 6 servings*

Hearty Pork Stew

2 pounds sweet potatoes, peeled and cut into 2-inch pieces (about 2 cups)
2 pounds boneless pork shoulder roast, cut into 1-inch pieces
1 can (14½ ounces) CAMPBELL'S® Chicken Gravy
1 teaspoon dried thyme leaves, crushed
½ teaspoon crushed red pepper
1 can (15 ounces) black-eyed peas, rinsed and drained

1. Put the potatoes in a 4- to 6-quart slow cooker. Top with the pork.

2. Stir the gravy, thyme, red pepper and peas in a small bowl. Pour over the pork and potatoes.

3. Cover and cook on LOW for 7 to 8 hours* or until the meat is fork-tender. *Makes 8 servings*

*Or on HIGH for 4 to 5 hours

Prep Time: 25 minutes • **Cook Time:** 7 to 8 hours

Potato Cheddar Soup

Weeknight Favorites

Turkey Ropa Vieja

12 ounces turkey tenderloin (2 large or 3 small) or boneless, skinless chicken thighs
1 can (8 ounces) tomato sauce
2 medium tomatoes, chopped
1 small onion, thinly sliced
1 small green bell pepper, chopped
4 pimiento-stuffed green olives, sliced
1 clove garlic, minced
¾ teaspoon ground cumin
½ teaspoon dried oregano
⅛ teaspoon black pepper
2 teaspoons lemon juice
¼ teaspoon salt
1 cup cooked brown rice (optional)
1 cup cooked black beans (optional)

1. Place turkey in slow cooker. Add tomato sauce, tomatoes, onion, bell pepper, olives, garlic, cumin, oregano and black pepper. Cover; cook on LOW 6 to 7 hours.

2. Shred turkey in slow cooker using 2 forks. Stir in lemon juice and salt. Serve with rice and black beans, if desired.   *Makes 4 servings*

Creamy Beef Stroganoff

2 cans (10¾ ounces **each**) CAMPBELL'S® Condensed Cream of
    Mushroom Soup (Regular, 98% Fat Free **or** 25% Less Sodium)
¼ cup water
2 tablespoons Worcestershire sauce
1 package (8 ounces) sliced white mushrooms
3 medium onions, coarsely chopped (about 1½ cups)
3 cloves garlic, minced
½ teaspoon ground black pepper
2 pounds boneless beef bottom round steak, sliced diagonally
    into strips
1 cup sour cream
    Hot cooked egg noodles
    Chopped fresh parsley (optional)

1. Stir the soup, water, Worcestershire sauce, mushrooms, onions, garlic and black pepper in a 6-quart slow cooker. Add the beef and stir to coat.

2. Cover and cook on LOW for 8 to 9 hours* or until the beef is cooked through.

3. Stir the sour cream into the cooker. Serve with the egg noodles. Top with the parsley, if desired.   *Makes 9 servings*

*Or on HIGH for 4 to 5 hours.

Prep Time: 15 minutes • **Cook Time:** 8 to 9 hours

Kitchen Tip

For more overall flavor and color, brown the beef before adding it to the slow cooker.

Creamy Beef Stroganoff

South-of-the-Border Cumin Chicken

1 package (16 ounces) frozen bell pepper stir-fry mixture, thawed
    or 3 bell peppers, thinly sliced*
4 chicken drumsticks, skin removed
4 chicken thighs, skin removed
1 can (about 14 ounces) stewed tomatoes
1 tablespoon green pepper sauce
2 teaspoons sugar
1¾ teaspoons ground cumin, divided
1¼ teaspoons salt
1 teaspoon dried oregano
¼ cup chopped fresh cilantro
1 to 2 medium limes, cut into wedges
    Hot cooked rice or corn tortilla chips

If using fresh bell peppers, add 1 small onion, chopped.

1. Place bell pepper mixture in slow cooker; arrange chicken on top of peppers.

2. Combine tomatoes, hot pepper sauce, sugar, 1 teaspoon cumin, salt and oregano in large bowl. Pour over chicken mixture. Cover; cook on LOW 8 hours or on HIGH 4 hours or until meat is just beginning to fall off bone.

3. Place chicken in shallow serving bowl. Stir remaining ¾ teaspoon cumin into tomato mixture; pour over chicken. Sprinkle with cilantro. Serve with lime wedges, cooked rice or tortilla chips.

Makes 4 servings

Editor's Note

Wake up your taste buds with this quick and simple chicken dish. This is the perfect recipe to start before work so you can come home to a delicious dinner.

South-of-the-Border Cumin Chicken

Caribbean Shrimp with Rice

1 package (12 ounces) medium frozen shrimp, thawed
½ cup chicken broth
1 clove garlic, minced
1 teaspoon chili powder
½ teaspoon salt
½ teaspoon dried oregano
1 cup frozen peas, thawed
½ cup diced tomatoes
2 cups cooked long-grain white rice

1. Combine shrimp, broth, garlic, chili powder, salt and oregano in slow cooker. Cover; cook on LOW 2 hours.

2. Add peas and tomatoes. Cover; cook on LOW 5 minutes.

3. Stir in rice. Cover; cook on LOW an additional 5 minutes.

Makes 4 servings

Prep Time: 10 minutes • **Cook Time:** 2 hours

Slow Cooker Stuffed Peppers

1 pound BOB EVANS® Original Recipe Sausage Roll
¾ cup instant rice
1 cup salsa
5 green peppers, tops removed, ribs and seeds cleaned out
2 cans (15 ounces each) tomato sauce

In medium skillet over medium heat, crumble and cook sausage until brown. Stir in rice and salsa. Stuff sausage mixture into green peppers. Place peppers into crock pot. Pour tomato sauce over peppers. Cover and cook on low 4 to 6 hours.

Makes 5 servings

Prep Time: 15 minutes • **Cook Time:** 4 to 6 hours

Caribbean Shrimp with Rice

Sicilian Steak Pinwheels

¾ pound mild or hot Italian sausage, casing removed
1¾ cups fresh bread crumbs
¾ cup grated Parmesan cheese
2 eggs
3 tablespoons minced parsley, plus additional for garnish
1½ to 2 pounds round steak
1 cup frozen peas
1 cup pasta sauce
1 cup beef broth

1. Coat 6-quart slow cooker with nonstick cooking spray. Mix sausage, bread crumbs, cheese, eggs and 3 tablespoons parsley in large bowl until well blended; set aside.

2. Place round steak between 2 large sheets plastic wrap. Pound steak with tenderizer mallet or back of skillet until meat is about ⅜ inch thick. Remove top layer of plastic wrap. Spread sausage mixture over steak. Press frozen peas into sausage mixture. Lift edge of plastic wrap at short end to begin rolling steak. Roll up completely. Tie at 2-inch intervals with kitchen string. Transfer to slow cooker.

3. Combine pasta sauce and broth in medium bowl. Pour over meat. Cover; cook on LOW 6 hours or until meat is tender and sausage is cooked through.

4. Transfer steak to serving platter; let stand 20 minutes. Remove string; slice. Meanwhile, skim and discard excess fat from sauce. Serve steak slices with sauce.   *Makes 4 to 6 servings*

Prep Time: 20 to 25 minutes • **Cook Time:** 6 hours

Sicilian Steak Pinwheels

Shredded Pork Burritos with Green Chile Sauce

1 tablespoon vegetable oil
1 large onion, chopped (about 1 cup)
4 cloves garlic, minced
2 jars (16 ounces **each**) PACE® Chunky Salsa
1 cup water
1 medium red pepper, chopped (about 1 cup)
8 green onions, chopped (about 1 cup)
1 bunch fresh cilantro leaves, chopped (about 1 cup)
¼ cup lemon pepper seasoning
¼ cup ground cumin
¼ cup chili powder
1 tablespoon lime juice
1 (4-pound) boneless pork loin roast, netted or tied
1 can (4 ounces) diced green chiles, drained
12 flour tortillas (10-inch), warmed
2 cups shredded Monterey Jack cheese (about 8 ounces)

1. Heat the oil in a 12-inch skillet over medium heat. Add the onion and garlic and cook until they're tender. Stir the salsa, water, red pepper, green onions, cilantro, lemon pepper, cumin, chili powder and lime juice in the skillet.

2. Place the pork into a 5-quart slow cooker. Pour the salsa mixture over the pork. Cover; cook on LOW for 8 to 9 hours or until the pork is fork-tender. Remove the pork from the cooker to a cutting board and let stand for 10 minutes. Using 2 forks, shred the pork.

3. Spoon 5 cups salsa mixture into a 2-quart saucepan. Stir in the chiles and cook over medium-high heat to a boil. Reduce the heat to low. Cook and stir for 15 minutes or until the mixture thickens.

4. Spoon 1 cup pork down the center of each tortilla. Top each with 2 tablespoons green chile sauce. Fold the sides of the tortillas over the filling and then fold up the ends to enclose the filling. Divide the remaining green chile sauce and the cheese over the burritos.

Makes 12 burritos

Coq au Vin

2 cups frozen pearl onions, thawed
4 slices thick-cut bacon, crisp-cooked and crumbled
1 cup sliced button mushrooms
1 clove garlic, minced
1 teaspoon dried thyme
⅛ teaspoon black pepper
6 boneless skinless chicken breasts (about 2 pounds)
½ cup dry red wine
¾ cup chicken broth
¼ cup tomato paste
3 tablespoons all-purpose flour
   Hot cooked egg noodles (optional)

1. Layer onions, bacon, mushrooms, garlic, thyme, pepper, chicken, wine and broth in slow cooker.

2. Cover; cook on LOW 6 to 8 hours.

3. Remove chicken and vegetables; cover and keep warm. Ladle ½ cup cooking liquid into small bowl; cool slightly. Mix reserved liquid, tomato paste and flour until smooth; stir into slow cooker. Cook; uncovered, on HIGH 15 minutes or until thickened. Serve over hot noodles, if desired.   *Makes 6 servings*

Prep Time: 15 minutes • **Cook Time:** 6 to 8 hours (LOW), plus 15 minutes (HIGH)

Editor's Note

Coq au Vin is a classic French dish that is made with chicken, salt pork or bacon, red wine and herbs. The dish originated when farmers needed a way to cook old chickens. A slow, moist cooking method was needed to tenderize the birds.

Ham with Fruited Bourbon Sauce

 1 bone-in ham, butt portion (about 6 pounds)
¾ cup packed dark brown sugar
½ cup raisins
½ cup apple juice
 1 teaspoon ground cinnamon
¼ teaspoon red pepper flakes
⅓ cup dried cherries
¼ cup cornstarch
¼ cup bourbon, rum, or apple juice

1. Coat 5-quart slow cooker with nonstick cooking spray. Add ham, cut side up. Combine brown sugar, raisins, apple juice, cinnamon and pepper flakes in small bowl; stir well. Pour mixture evenly over ham. Cover; cook on LOW 9 to 10 hours or on HIGH 4½ to 5 hours. Add cherries 30 minutes before end of cooking time.

2. Transfer ham to cutting board. Let stand 15 minutes before slicing.

3. Pour cooking liquid into large measuring cup and let stand 5 minutes. Skim and discard excess fat. Return cooking liquid to slow cooker.

4. Turn slow cooker to HIGH. Whisk cornstarch and bourbon in small bowl until cornstarch is dissolved. Stir into cooking liquid. Cover; cook on HIGH 15 to 20 minutes longer or until thickened. Serve sauce over sliced ham.   *Makes 10 to 12 servings*

Prep Time: 5 minutes • **Cook Time:** 9 to 10 hours (LOW) or 4½ to 5 hours (HIGH)

Kitchen Tip

If the words "natural juices added" or "added water" appear on the ham label, that means you are paying for the weight of these fillers and getting less meat per pound.

Ham With Fruited Bourbon Sauce

Osso Bucco

1 large onion, cut into thin wedges
2 large carrots, sliced
4 cloves garlic, sliced
4 veal shanks (3 to 4 pounds)
2 teaspoons herbes de Provence*
1 teaspoon salt
½ teaspoon black pepper
¾ cup beef broth or consommé
¼ cup dry vermouth (optional)
3 tablespoons all-purpose flour
3 tablespoons water
¼ cup minced fresh parsley
1 small clove garlic, minced
1 teaspoon grated lemon peel

(Or substitute ½ teaspoon each dried thyme, rosemary, oregano and basil)

1. Coat slow cooker with cooking spray. Place onion, carrots and sliced garlic in bottom of slow cooker. Arrange veal over vegetables, overlapping slightly. Sprinkle with herbes de Provence, salt and pepper. Add broth and vermouth, if desired. Cover; cook on LOW 8 to 9 hours or HIGH 5 to 6 hours until veal and vegetables are tender.

2. Transfer veal and vegetables to serving platter. Cover with foil to keep warm. Turn slow cooker to HIGH. Combine flour and water in small bowl until smooth. Stir into slow cooker. Cook, uncovered, 15 minutes or until sauce thickens.

3. Combine parsley, minced garlic and lemon peel in small bowl. Serve veal with sauce and sprinkle with parsley mixture.

Makes 4 servings

Osso Bucco

Chicken Teriyaki

1 pound boneless skinless chicken tenders
1 can (6 ounces) pineapple juice
¼ cup soy sauce
1 tablespoon sugar
1 tablespoon minced fresh ginger
1 tablespoon minced garlic
1 tablespoon vegetable oil
1 tablespoon molasses
24 cherry tomatoes (optional)
2 cups hot cooked rice

Combine all ingredients except rice in slow cooker. Cover; cook on LOW 2 hours or until chicken is tender. Serve chicken and sauce over rice.

Makes 4 servings

Slow Cooker Sweet and Sour Brats

1 package (19 ounces) BOB EVANS® Original Brats, cut into bite size pieces
1 package (16 ounces) frozen vegetables for stir fry
1 can (20 ounces) unsweetened pineapple chunks, drained, reserve ¼ cup juice
1 cup barbecue sauce
2 tablespoons soy sauce
1 tablespoon cider vinegar
2 tablespoons cornstarch
3 cups hot cooked rice

In nonstick skillet over medium heat, brown brats. Place in crock pot and top with vegetables and pineapple. In small bowl combine BBQ sauce, soy sauce, vinegar, cornstarch and reserved pineapple juice. Pour over vegetables and pineapple in crock pot. Cover and cook on low 4 to 6 hours. Stir before serving and serve with rice.

Makes 4 to 6 servings

Prep Time: 15 minutes • **Cook Time:** 4 to 6 hours

Chicken Teriyaki

Yankee Pot Roast and Vegetables

3 unpeeled medium baking potatoes (about 1 pound), cut into quarters
2 large carrots, cut into ¾-inch slices
2 stalks celery, cut into ¾-inch slices
1 medium onion, sliced
1 large parsnip, cut into ¾-inch slices
2 bay leaves
1 teaspoon dried rosemary
½ teaspoon dried thyme
1 beef chuck pot roast (2½ pounds)
   Salt and black pepper
½ cup beef broth

1. Combine vegetables, bay leaves, rosemary and thyme in slow cooker.

2. Trim and discard excess fat from beef. Cut beef into serving-size pieces; sprinkle with salt and pepper. Place beef over vegetables. Pour broth over beef. Cover; cook on LOW 8½ to 9 hours or until beef is fork-tender.

3. Transfer beef to serving platter. Arrange vegetables around beef. Remove and discard bay leaves.   *Makes 10 to 12 servings*

Prep Time: 10 minutes • **Cook Time:** 8½ to 9 hours

Kitchen Tip

To make gravy, ladle the juices into a 2-cup measure; let stand 5 minutes. Skim off and discard fat. Measure remaining juices and heat to a boil in small saucepan. For each cup of juice, mix 2 tablespoons flour with ¼ cup cold water until smooth. Add mixture to boiling juices; cook and stir constantly for 1 minute or until thickened.

Yankee Pot Roast and Vegetables

Cheesy Shrimp on Grits

      1 cup finely chopped green bell pepper
      1 cup finely chopped red bell pepper
   ½ cup thinly sliced celery
      1 bunch green onions, chopped, divided
      4 tablespoons (½ stick) butter, cubed
  1¼ teaspoons seafood seasoning
      2 bay leaves
   ¼ teaspoon ground red pepper
      1 pound medium raw shrimp, peeled and deveined
  5⅓ cups water
  1⅓ cups quick-cooking grits
      8 ounces shredded sharp Cheddar cheese
   ¼ cup whipping cream or half-and-half

1. Coat slow cooker with nonstick cooking spray. Add bell peppers, celery, all but ½ cup green onions, butter, seafood seasoning, bay leaves and red pepper. Cover; cook on LOW 4 hours or on HIGH 2 hours.

2. Turn slow cooker to HIGH. Add shrimp. Cover; cook 15 minutes. Meanwhile, prepare grits according to package directions.

3. Discard bay leaves from shrimp mixture. Stir in cheese, cream and reserved ½ cup green onions. Cook 5 minutes or until cheese has melted. Serve over grits. *Makes 6 servings*

Variation: This dish is also delicious served over polenta.

Prep Time: 15 minutes • **Cook Time:** 4 hours (LOW) or 2 hours (HIGH) plus 20 minutes (HIGH)

Cheesy Shrimp on Grits

Moroccan-Style Lamb Shoulder Chops with Couscous

4 lamb blade chops (about 2½ pounds)
   Salt and black pepper
1 tablespoon olive oil
1 onion, chopped
1 clove garlic, minced
1 teaspoon grated fresh ginger
¼ teaspoon ground cinnamon
½ teaspoon ground turmeric
½ teaspoon salt
¼ teaspoon black pepper
1 bay leaf
1 can (about 14 ounces) diced tomatoes
1 cup canned chickpeas, rinsed and drained
½ cup water
2 tablespoons lemon juice
   Hot couscous
   Lemon wedges (optional)

1. Coat 5- to 6-quart slow cooker with nonstick cooking spray. Season lamb chops with salt and pepper. Heat oil in large skillet over medium-high heat. Add lamb chops; brown on all sides. Transfer to slow cooker.

2. Add onion to skillet; cook and stir 2 to 3 minutes or until translucent. Add garlic, ginger, cinnamon, turmeric, salt, ¼ teaspoon pepper and bay leaf; cook and stir 30 seconds longer. Stir in tomatoes, chickpeas, water and lemon juice; simmer 2 minutes. Pour mixture over lamb. Cover; cook on HIGH 3½ to 4 hours or until lamb is tender.

3. Serve lamb chops over coucous with sauce and vegetables. Serve with lemon wedges.   *Makes 4 servings*

Prep Time: 15 minutes • **Cook Time:** 3½ to 4 hours

Greek Chicken Pitas with Creamy Mustard Sauce

Filling
- 1 medium green bell pepper, sliced into ½-inch strips
- 1 medium onion, cut into 8 wedges
- 1 pound boneless skinless chicken breasts
- 1 tablespoon olive oil
- 2 teaspoons dried Greek seasoning blend
- ¼ teaspoon salt

Sauce
- ¼ cup plain yogurt
- ¼ cup mayonnaise
- 1 tablespoon prepared mustard
- ¼ teaspoon salt
- 4 whole pita rounds
- ½ cup crumbled feta cheese
  - Optional toppings: sliced cucumbers, sliced tomatoes, kalamata olives

1. Coat slow cooker with nonstick cooking spray; add bell pepper and onion. Add chicken and drizzle with oil. Sprinkle evenly with Greek seasoning and ¼ teaspoon salt. Cover; cook on HIGH 3 to 4 hours or until chicken is no longer pink in center.

2. Remove chicken and slice. Remove vegetables using slotted spoon.

3. Combine yogurt, mayonnaise, mustard and ¼ teaspoon salt in small bowl. Whisk until smooth.

4. Warm pitas according to package directions. Cut in half; fill with chicken, sauce, vegetables and feta cheese. Serve with toppings.

Makes 4 servings

Prep Time: 10 minutes • **Cook Time:** 3 to 4 hours

Bistro-Style Short Ribs

Vegetable cooking spray
3 pounds beef short ribs, cut into individual rib pieces
1 large onion, chopped (about 1 cup)
2 medium carrots, chopped (about ⅔ cup)
1 stalk celery, chopped (about ½ cup)
2¾ cups PREGO® Traditional Italian Sauce
1¾ cups SWANSON® Beef Stock

1. Spray a 6-quart oven-safe saucepot with the cooking spray and heat over medium-high heat for 1 minute. Add the ribs in 2 batches and cook until they're browned on all sides. Remove the ribs from the saucepot. Pour off all but **2 tablespoons** fat.

2. Add the onion, carrots and celery to the saucepot and cook until they're tender. Stir the sauce and stock in the saucepot and heat to a boil. Return the ribs to the saucepot. Cover the saucepot.

3. Bake at 350°F. for 1 hour 30 minutes or until the ribs are fork-tender. *Makes 4 servings*

Prep Time: 10 minutes • **Cook Time:** 15 minutes •
Bake Time: 1 hour, 30 minutes

Bistro-Style Short Ribs

Chipotle Cornish Hens

3 small carrots, cut into ½-inch rounds
3 stalks celery, cut into ½-inch pieces
1 onion, chopped
1 can (7 ounces) chipotle peppers in adobo sauce, divided
2 cups prepared corn bread stuffing*
4 Cornish hens (about 1½ pounds each)
   Salt and black pepper
   Fresh parsley, chopped (optional)

1. Coat 5- to 6-quart slow cooker with nonstick cooking spray. Add carrots, celery and onion.

2. Pour canned chipotles into small bowl. Finely chop ½ chipotle pepper and mix into prepared stuffing. Remove remaining peppers from adobo sauce and reserve for another use. Finely chop remaining ½ chipotle pepper and add to adobo sauce.*

3. Season hens with salt and black pepper inside and out. Fill each hen with about ½ cup stuffing. Rub adobo sauce onto hens. Arrange hens in slow cooker, necks down, legs up. Cover; cook on HIGH 3½ to 4 hours or until no longer pink near bone.

4. Transfer hens to serving platter. Remove vegetables with slotted spoon and arrange around hens. Garnish with parsley. Spoon cooking juices over hens and vegetables, if desired.   *Makes 4 servings*

*For spicier flavor, use 1 chipotle pepper in stuffing and 1 chipotle pepper in sauce.

Prep Time: 15 minutes • **Cook Time:** 3½ to 4 hours

Chipotle Cornish Hens

Spinach and Ricotta Stuffed Shells

1 package (16 ounces) jumbo pasta shells
1 package (16 ounces) ricotta cheese
7 ounces frozen chopped spinach, thawed and well-drained
½ cup grated Parmesan cheese
1 egg, lightly beaten
1 clove garlic, minced
½ teaspoon salt
1 jar (26 ounces) marinara sauce
½ cup shredded mozzarella cheese
1 teaspoon olive oil

1. Cook pasta shells according to package directions; drain. Stir together ricotta, spinach, Parmesan, egg, garlic and salt.

2. Pour ¼ cup marinara sauce into slow cooker. Spoon 2 to 3 tablespoons of ricotta mixture into 1 pasta shell and place, filling side down, in bottom of slow cooker. Repeat with enough additional shells to cover bottom of slow cooker in single layer. Top with another ¼ cup marinara sauce. Repeat layers using all remaining pasta shells and filling. Top with any remaining marinara sauce and sprinkle with mozzarella cheese. Drizzle with olive oil.

3. Cover; cook on HIGH 3 to 4 hours or until mozzarella is melted and sauce is bubbly and heated through.   *Makes 4 to 6 servings*

Prep Time: 45 minutes • **Cook Time:** 3 to 4 hours

Editor's Note

Tired of take-out pizza and fast food? Indulge your family with a comforting slow-cooked Italian casserole tonight!

Spinach and Ricotta Stuffed Shells

Polska Kielbasa with Beer & Onions

18 ounces brown ale or beer
⅓ cup packed dark brown sugar
⅓ cup honey mustard
2 kielbasa sausages (16 ounces each), cut into 4-inch pieces
2 onions, quartered

Combine ale, brown sugar and honey mustard in slow cooker. Add sausage pieces. Top with onions. Cover; cook on LOW 4 to 5 hours, stirring occasionally. *Makes 6 to 8 servings*

Prep Time: 10 minutes • **Cook Time:** 4 to 5 hours

Sloppy Sloppy Joes

4 pounds ground beef
1 cup chopped onion
1 cup chopped green bell pepper
1 can (about 28 ounces) tomato sauce
2 cans (10¾ ounces each) condensed tomato soup, undiluted
1 cup packed brown sugar
¼ cup ketchup
3 tablespoons Worcestershire sauce
1 tablespoon dry mustard
1 tablespoon prepared mustard
1½ teaspoons chili powder
1 teaspoon garlic powder
  Toasted hamburger buns

1. Brown beef 6 to 8 minutes in large skillet over medium-high heat, stirring to break up meat; drain fat. Add onion and bell pepper; cook and stir 5 to 10 minutes or until onion is translucent.

2. Transfer beef mixture to 4- to 5-quart slow cooker. Add remaining ingredients except buns; stir until well blended.

3. Cover; cook on LOW 4 to 6 hours. Serve on buns.
Makes 16 servings

Polska Kielbasa with Beer & Onions

Greek Chicken and Orzo

2 medium green bell peppers, cut into thin strips
1 cup chopped onion
2 teaspoons olive oil
8 skinless chicken thighs, rinsed and patted dry
1 tablespoon dried oregano
¾ teaspoon salt, divided
½ teaspoon dried rosemary
½ teaspoon garlic powder
½ teaspoon black pepper, divided
8 ounces uncooked orzo pasta
½ cup water
  Grated peel and juice of 1 lemon
2 ounces crumbled feta cheese (optional)
  Chopped fresh parsley (optional)

1. Coat 6-quart slow cooker with nonstick cooking spray. Add bell peppers and onion.

2. Heat oil in large skillet over medium-high heat. Brown chicken on both sides. Transfer to slow cooker, overlapping slightly if necessary. Sprinkle chicken with oregano, ¼ teaspoon salt, rosemary, garlic powder and ¼ teaspoon black pepper. Cover; cook on LOW 5 to 6 hours or on HIGH 3 hours.

3. Transfer chicken to plate. Turn slow cooker to HIGH. Stir orzo, water, lemon peel, lemon juice and remaining ½ teaspoon salt and ¼ teaspoon black pepper into slow cooker. Top with chicken. Cover; cook 30 minutes or until pasta is done. Garnish with feta cheese and parsley.   *Makes 4 servings*

Note: To remove chicken skin easily, grasp skin with paper towel and pull away. Repeat with fresh paper towel for each piece of chicken, discarding skins and towels.

Prep Time: 5 minutes • **Cook Time:** 5 to 6 hours (LOW) or 3½ hours (HIGH)

Greek Chicken and Orzo

Bountiful Brunch

Wake-Up Potato and Sausage Breakfast Casserole

   1 pound kielbasa or smoked sausage, diced
   1 cup chopped onion
   1 cup chopped red bell pepper
   1 package (20 ounces) refrigerated Southwestern-style
       hash browns
10 eggs
   1 cup milk
   1 cup shredded Monterey Jack or sharp Cheddar cheese

1. Coat slow cooker with nonstick cooking spray. Heat large skillet over medium-high heat. Cook and stir sausage and onion until sausage is browned. Drain fat. Stir in bell pepper.

2. Place ⅓ of potatoes in slow cooker. Top with ½ of sausage mixture. Repeat layers ending with potatoes.

3. Whisk eggs and milk in medium bowl. Pour evenly over potatoes. Cover; cook on LOW 6 to 7 hours.

4. Turn off slow cooker. Sprinkle casserole with cheese; let stand 10 minutes or until cheese is melted.   *Makes 8 servings*

Prep Time: 15 minutes • **Cook Time:** 6 to 7 hours

French Toast Bread Pudding

2 tablespoons packed dark brown sugar
2½ teaspoons ground cinnamon
1 loaf (24 ounces) thick-sliced white bread
2 cups whipping cream
2 cups half-and-half
2 teaspoons vanilla
¼ teaspoon salt
4 egg yolks
1¼ cups granulated sugar
¼ teaspoon ground nutmeg
   Maple syrup
   Whipped cream (optional)

1. Coat slow cooker with nonstick cooking spray. Combine brown sugar and cinnamon in small bowl. Reserve 1 tablespoon; set aside.

2. Cut bread slices in half diagonally. Arrange bread slices in single layer in bottom of slow cooker, keeping as flat as possible. Evenly sprinkle with cinnamon mixture. Repeat layering, keeping layers as flat as possible.

3. Cook and stir cream, half-and-half, vanilla and salt in large saucepan over medium heat, allowing mixture to come to a boil. Reduce heat to low.

4. Whisk egg yolks and granulated sugar in medium bowl on damp towel to prevent slipping. Continue to whisk quickly while adding ¼ cup of hot cream mixture. Add warmed egg mixture to saucepan and increase heat to medium-high. Cook and stir about 5 minutes or until mixture thickens slightly. *Do not boil.*

5. Remove from heat and stir in nutmeg. Pour mixture over bread and press bread down lightly. Sprinkle reserved cinnamon mixture on top. Cover; cook on LOW 3 to 4 hours or on HIGH 1½ to 2 hours or until toothpick inserted into center comes out clean.

continued on page 84

French Toast Bread Pudding

French Toast Bread Pudding, continued

6. Turn off slow cooker and uncover. Let pudding rest 10 minutes. Serve with maple syrup and whipped cream, if desired.

Makes 6 to 8 servings

Prep Time: 15 minutes • **Cook Time:** 3 to 4 hours (LOW) or 1½ to 2 hours (HIGH)

Spicy Apple Butter

5 pounds tart cooking apples (McIntosh or Granny Smith), peeled, cored and quartered (about 10 large apples)
1 cup sugar
½ cup apple juice
2 teaspoons ground cinnamon
½ teaspoon ground cloves
½ teaspoon ground allspice

1. Combine all ingredients in slow cooker. Cover; cook on LOW 8 to 10 hours or until apples are very tender.

2. Mash apples with potato masher. Cook, uncovered, on LOW 2 hours or until thickened, stirring occasionally to prevent sticking.

Makes about 6 cups

Serving Suggestion: Homemade apple butter is a great as an alternative to store-bought jam or jelly on your favorite toast or muffin. For an instant dessert, try toasting a few slices of pound cake and spreading them with apple butter!

Prep Time: 25 minutes • **Cook Time:** 10 to 12 hours

Spicy Apple Butter

Oatmeal Crème Brûlée

4 cups water
3 cups uncooked quick-cooking oats
½ teaspoon salt
6 egg yolks
½ cup granulated sugar
2 cups whipping cream
1 teaspoon vanilla
¼ cup packed light brown sugar
Fresh berries (optional)

1. Coat slow cooker with nonstick cooking spray. Cover and set on HIGH to heat. Meanwhile, bring water to a boil. Immediately pour into preheated slow cooker. Stir in oats and salt. Cover.

2. Combine egg yolks and granulated sugar in small bowl. Heat cream and vanilla in medium saucepan over medium heat until mixture begins to simmer. *Do not boil.* Remove from heat. Whisk ½ cup hot cream into yolks, stirring rapidly so yolks don't cook.* Whisk warmed egg mixture into cream, stirring rapidly to blend well. Spoon mixture over oatmeal. Do not stir.

3. Turn slow cooker to LOW. Line lid with 2 paper towels. Cover; cook on LOW 3 to 3½ hours or until custard is set.

4. Uncover and sprinkle brown sugar over surface of custard. Line lid with 2 dry paper towels. Cover; continue cooking on LOW 10 to 15 minutes or until brown sugar has melted. Serve with fresh berries, if desired.

Makes 4 to 6 servings

*Place bowl on damp towel to prevent slipping.

Prep Time: 15 minutes • **Cook Time:** 3 to 3½ hours

Oatmeal Crème Brûlée

Bacon and Cheese Brunch Potatoes

3 medium russet potatoes (about 2 pounds), peeled and cut into
    1-inch dice
1 cup chopped onion
½ teaspoon seasoned salt
4 slices bacon, crisp-cooked and crumbled
1 cup (4 ounces) shredded sharp Cheddar cheese
1 tablespoon water or chicken broth

1. Coat 4-quart slow cooker with cooking spray. Place half of potatoes in slow cooker. Sprinkle ½ of onion and seasoned salt over potatoes; top with ½ of bacon and cheese. Repeat layers, ending with cheese. Sprinkle water over top.

2. Cover; cook on LOW 6 hours or on HIGH 3½ hours until potatoes and onion are tender. Stir gently to mix. *Makes 6 servings*

Prep Time: 10 minutes • **Cook Time:** 6 hours (LOW) or 3½ hours (HIGH)

Kitchen Tip

Removing fat from the skillet as bacon cooks will reduce splattering and produces crisper bacon. A turkey baster is the perfect tool to remove fat from the skillet.

Bacon and Cheese Brunch Potatoes

Apple and Granola Breakfast Cobbler

4 Granny Smith apples, peeled, cored and sliced
2 cups granola cereal, plus additional for garnish
½ cup packed light brown sugar
2 tablespoons butter, cut into small pieces
1 tablespoon lemon juice
1 teaspoon ground cinnamon
   Cream, half-and-half or vanilla yogurt (optional)

1. Combine apples, granola, brown sugar, butter, lemon juice and cinnamon in slow cooker.

2. Cover; cook on LOW 6 hours or on HIGH 2 to 3 hours. Serve hot with additional granola sprinkled on top. Serve with cream.

Makes 4 servings

Prep Time: 5 minutes • **Cook Time:** 6 hours (LOW) or 2 to 3 hours (HIGH)

Viennese Coffee

3 cups strong freshly brewed hot coffee
3 tablespoons chocolate syrup
1 teaspoon sugar
⅓ cup whipping cream
¼ cup crème de cacao or Irish cream liqueur (optional)
   Whipped cream (optional)
   Chocolate shavings (optional)

1. Combine coffee, chocolate syrup and sugar in slow cooker. Cover; cook on LOW 2 to 2½ hours. Stir in whipping cream and crème de cacao, if desired. Cover; cook 30 minutes or until heated through.

2. Ladle coffee into coffee cups; top with whipped cream and chocolate shavings.

Makes about 4 servings

Apple and Granola Breakfast Cobbler

Orange Cranberry-Nut Bread

  2 cups all-purpose flour
½ cup chopped pecans
  1 teaspoon baking powder
½ teaspoon baking soda
¼ teaspoon salt
  1 cup dried cranberries
  2 teaspoons dried orange peel
⅔ cup boiling water
¾ cup sugar
  2 tablespoons shortening
  1 egg, lightly beaten
  1 teaspoon vanilla

1. Coat slow cooker with nonstick cooking spray. Combine flour, pecans, baking powder, baking soda and salt in medium bowl.

2. Combine cranberries and orange peel in large bowl; pour boiling water over fruit mixture and stir; let stand 5 minutes. Add sugar, shortening, egg and vanilla; stir just until blended. Add flour mixture; stir just until blended.

3. Pour batter into slow cooker. Cover; cook on HIGH 1¼ to 1½ hours or until edges begin to brown and toothpick inserted into center comes out clean. Remove stoneware from slow cooker. Cool on wire rack 10 minutes. Remove bread from stoneware; cool completely.

Makes 8 to 10 servings

Prep Time: 15 minutes • **Cook Time:** 1¼ to 1½ hours

Cheese Grits with Chiles and Bacon

6 strips bacon, divided
1 serrano or jalapeño pepper,* cored, seeded and minced
1 large shallot or small onion, finely chopped
4 cups chicken broth
1 cup grits**
¼ teaspoon black pepper
  Salt, to taste
1 cup (4 ounces) shredded Cheddar cheese
½ cup half-and-half
2 tablespoons finely chopped green onion

Hot peppers can sting and irritate the skin, so wear rubber gloves when handling peppers and do not touch eyes.

**You may use coarse, instant, yellow or stone-ground grits.*

1. Cook bacon on both sides in medium skillet until crisp; drain on paper towels. Cut 2 strips into bite-size pieces. Refrigerate and reserve remaining bacon. Place cut-up bacon in slow cooker.

2. Drain all but 1 tablespoon bacon drippings from skillet. Add pepper and shallot; cook and stir over medium-high heat 1 minute or until shallot is transparent and lightly browned. Transfer to slow cooker. Stir in broth, grits, pepper and salt. Cover; cook on LOW 4 hours.

3. Stir in cheese and half-and-half. Sprinkle with green onion. Chop remaining bacon into bite-size pieces and sprinkle on top of each serving. Serve immediately.   *Makes 4 servings*

Prep Time: 15 minutes • **Cook Time:** 4 hours

Ham and Cheddar Brunch Strata

8 ounces French bread, torn into small pieces
2 cups shredded sharp Cheddar cheese, divided
1½ cups diced ham
½ cup finely chopped green onions, divided
4 large eggs
1 cup half-and-half or whole milk
1 tablespoon Worcestershire sauce
⅛ teaspoon ground red pepper

1. Coat slow cooker with nonstick cooking spray. Cut parchment paper to fit bottom of stoneware* and press into place. Spray paper lightly with nonstick cooking spray.

2. Layer bread, 1½ cups cheese, ham and all but 2 tablespoons green onions in slow cooker.

3. Whisk eggs, half-and-half, Worcestershire sauce and red pepper in small bowl. Pour evenly into slow cooker. Cover; cook on LOW 3½ hours or until knife inserted into center comes out clean.

4. Turn off slow cooker. Sprinkle evenly with reserved ½ cup cheese and 2 tablespoons green onions. Cover; let stand 10 minutes or until cheese is melted.

5. Run knife or rubber spatula around outer edges, lifting bottom slightly. Invert onto plate and peel off paper. Invert again onto serving plate. *Makes 6 to 8 servings*

*To cut parchment paper to fit, trace around the stoneware bottom, then cut the paper slightly smaller to fit. If parchment paper is unavailable, substitute waxed paper.

Prep Time: 10 minutes • **Cook Time:** 3½ hours

Ham and Cheddar Brunch Strata

Apple-Cinnamon Breakfast Risotto

4 tablespoons (½ stick) butter
4 medium Granny Smith apples, peeled, cored and diced into
    ½-inch cubes (about 1½ pounds)
1½ teaspoons ground cinnamon
 ¼ teaspoon salt
 ¼ teaspoon ground allspice
1½ cups arborio rice
 ½ cup packed dark brown sugar
4 cups apple juice, at room temperature
1 teaspoon vanilla

1. Coat slow cooker with nonstick cooking spray. Melt butter in large skillet over medium-high heat. Add apples, cinnamon, salt and allspice. Cook and stir 3 to 5 minutes or until apples begin to release juices. Transfer to slow cooker.

2. Add rice and stir to coat. Sprinkle brown sugar evenly over top. Add apple juice and vanilla. Cover; cook on HIGH 1½ to 2 hours or until all liquid is absorbed. Ladle risotto into bowls and serve hot. Garnish as desired.   *Makes 6 servings*

Prep Time: 10 minutes • **Cook Time:** 1½ to 2 hours

Editor's Note

Switch up your morning routine by exchanging a bowl of oatmeal for this delicious breakfast treat.

Apple-Cinnamon Breakfast Risotto

Savory Sausage Bread Pudding

4 eggs
2 cups milk or 1 cup half-and-half and 1 cup milk
¼ teaspoon salt
¼ teaspoon black pepper
¼ teaspoon dried thyme
⅛ teaspoon red pepper flakes
1 package (10 ounces) smoked breakfast sausage links, cut into
  ½-inch pieces
2 cups day-old bread cubes, cut into ½-inch pieces
¾ cup (3 ounces) shredded Cheddar cheese

1. Beat eggs in large bowl. Add milk, salt, black pepper, thyme and red pepper flakes; stir well. Stir in sausage, bread and cheese. Press bread into egg mixture. Set aside 10 minutes or until bread has absorbed liquid.

2. Generously butter 2-quart baking dish that fits inside 5- or 6-quart slow cooker. Pour sausage mixture into dish. Cover dish with buttered foil, butter side down.

3. Pour 1 inch hot water into slow cooker. Add baking dish. Cover; cook on LOW 4 to 5 hours or until toothpick inserted into center comes out clean. *Makes 4 to 6 servings*

Prep Time: 10 minutes • **Cook Time:** 4 to 5 hours

Kitchen Tip

For a time saver in the morning, prepare the casserole the night before. Cover and refrigerate until ready to cook.

Savory Sausage Bread Pudding

Cinnamon Latté

6 cups double-strength brewed coffee*
2 cups half-and-half
1 cup sugar
1 teaspoon vanilla
3 cinnamon sticks, plus additional for garnish
   Whipped cream (optional)

*Double the amount of coffee grounds normally used to brew coffee. Or substitute 8 teaspoons instant coffee dissolved in 6 cups boiling water.

1. Blend coffee, half-and-half, sugar and vanilla in slow cooker. Add cinnamon sticks. Cover; cook on HIGH 3 hours.

2. Remove cinnamon sticks. Serve latté in tall coffee mugs with dollop of whipped cream and cinnamon stick, if desired.

Makes 6 to 8 servings

Prep Time: 5 minutes • **Cook Time:** 3 hours

Editor's Note

Really impress your brunch guests with this delicious café-style coffee treat. Store leftover Cinnamon Latté in the refrigerator and serve over ice for a refreshing creamy beverage.

Cinnamon Latté

Orange Date-Nut Bread

2 cups all-purpose unbleached flour plus additional for dusting
½ cup chopped pecans
1 teaspoon baking powder
½ teaspoon baking soda
¼ teaspoon salt
1 cup chopped dates
2 teaspoons dried orange peel
⅔ cup boiling water
¾ cup sugar
2 tablespoons shortening
1 egg, lightly beaten
1 teaspoon vanilla

1. Spray 1-quart high-sided casserole with nonstick cooking spray; dust with flour.

2. Combine flour, pecans, baking powder, baking soda and salt in medium bowl.

3. Combine dates and orange peel in large bowl; pour boiling water over date mixture; let stand 5 minutes. Add sugar, shortening, egg and vanilla; stir just until blended.

4. Add flour mixture to date mixture; stir just until blended. Pour batter into prepared dish; place in slow cooker. Cover; cook on HIGH 2½ hours or until edges begin to brown.

5. Remove dish from slow cooker. Cool on wire rack 10 minutes. Remove bread to wire rack; cool completely.

Makes 8 to 10 servings

Orange Date-Nut Bread

Savory Side Dishes

No-Fuss Macaroni & Cheese

2 cups (about 8 ounces) uncooked elbow macaroni
4 ounces pasteurized processed cheese, cubed
1 cup (4 ounces) shredded mild Cheddar cheese
½ teaspoon salt
⅛ teaspoon black pepper
1½ cups milk

Combine macaroni, cheeses, salt and pepper in slow cooker. Pour milk over top. Cover; cook on LOW 2 to 3 hours, stirring after 20 to 30 minutes.

Makes 6 to 8 servings

Kitchen Tip: As with all macaroni and cheese dishes, as it sits, the cheese sauce thickens and begins to dry out. If it dries out, stir in a little extra milk and heat through. Do not cook longer than 4 hours.

Note: This is a simple way to make macaroni and cheese without taking the time to boil water and cook noodles. Kids can even make this one on their own.

Prep Time: 10 minutes • **Cook Time:** 2 to 3 hours

Orange-Spiced Sweet Potatoes

2 pounds sweet potatoes, peeled and diced
½ cup dark brown sugar, packed
½ cup butter (1 stick), cut into small pieces
1 teaspoon ground cinnamon
½ teaspoon ground nutmeg
½ teaspoon grated orange peel
    Juice of 1 medium orange
¼ teaspoon salt
1 teaspoon vanilla
    Chopped toasted pecans (optional)

Place all ingredients, except pecans, in slow cooker. Cover; cook on LOW 4 hours or on HIGH 2 hours until potatoes are tender. Sprinkle with pecans before serving. *Makes 8 servings*

Variation: Mash sweet potatoes with a hand masher or electric mixer; add ¼ cup milk or whipping cream for a moister consistency. Sprinkle with a mixture of sugar and ground cinnamon.

Cheesy Corn and Peppers

2 pounds frozen corn kernels
2 tablespoons butter, cubed
2 poblano chile peppers, chopped
1 teaspoon salt
½ teaspoon ground cumin
¼ teaspoon black pepper
1 cup (4 ounces) shredded sharp Cheddar cheese
3 ounces cream cheese, cubed

1. Coat slow cooker with nonstick cooking spray. Add corn, butter, chile peppers, salt, cumin and black pepper.

2. Cover; cook on HIGH for 2 hours. Add cheeses; stir to blend. Cook 15 minutes or until cheeses are melted. *Makes 8 servings*

Prep Time: 8 minutes • **Cook Time:** 2¼ hours

Orange-Spiced Sweet Potatoes

Simmered Red Beans with Rice

2 cans (about 15 ounces each) red beans, rinsed and drained
1 can (about 14 ounces) diced tomatoes, undrained
½ cup *each* chopped celery, green bell pepper and green onions
2 cloves garlic, minced
1 to 2 teaspoons hot pepper sauce
1 teaspoon Worcestershire sauce
1 bay leaf
Hot cooked rice

1. Combine all ingredients, except rice, in slow cooker. Cover; cook on LOW 4 to 6 hours or HIGH 2 to 3 hours.

2. Remove and discard bay leaf. Slightly mash mixture in slow cooker with potato masher to thicken. Cover; cook on LOW 30 to 60 minutes. Serve over rice. *Makes 6 servings*

Slow Cooker Cheddar Polenta

7 cups hot water
2 cups polenta (not "quick-cooking") or coarse-ground yellow cornmeal
2 tablespoons extra-virgin olive oil
2 teaspoons salt
3 cups grated CABOT® Extra Sharp or Sharp Cheddar (about 12 ounces)

1. Combine water, polenta, olive oil and salt in slow cooker; whisk until well blended. Add cheese and whisk again.

2. Cover and cook on HIGH setting for 2 hours or until most liquid is absorbed. Stir well. (Polenta should have consistency of thick cooked cereal.) *Makes 8 servings*

Note: If not serving right away, pour onto oiled baking sheet with sides, spreading into even layer; cover with plastic wrap and let cool. When ready to serve, cut into rectangles and sauté in nonstick skillet with olive oil until golden on both sides.

Simmered Red Beans with Rice

Scalloped Tomatoes & Corn

1 can (15 ounces) cream-style corn
1 can (about 14 ounces) diced tomatoes, undrained
¾ cup saltine cracker crumbs
1 egg, lightly beaten
2 teaspoons sugar
¾ teaspoon black pepper
Chopped fresh tomatoes (optional)
Chopped fresh parsley (optional)

Combine corn, diced tomatoes, cracker crumbs, egg, sugar and pepper in slow cooker; mix well. Cover; cook on LOW 4 to 6 hours. Sprinkle with fresh tomatoes and parsley before serving, if desired.

Makes 4 to 6 servings

Prep Time: 7 minutes • **Cook Time:** 4 to 6 hours

Easy Dirty Rice

½ pound bulk Italian sausage
2 cups water
1 cup uncooked long grain rice
1 large onion, finely chopped
1 large green bell pepper, finely chopped
½ cup finely chopped celery
1½ teaspoons salt
½ teaspoon ground red pepper
½ cup chopped fresh parsley

1. Brown sausage in skillet 6 to 8 minutes over medium-high heat, stirring to break up meat; drain fat. Place into slow cooker.

2. Stir in all remaining ingredients except parsley. Cover; cook on LOW 2 hours. Stir in parsley.

Makes 4 servings

Scalloped Tomatoes & Corn

Braised Sweet and Sour Cabbage and Apples

2 tablespoons unsalted butter
6 cups coarsely shredded red cabbage
1 large sweet apple, peeled, cored and cut into bite-size pieces
½ cup raisins
½ cup apple cider
3 tablespoons cider vinegar, divided
2 tablespoons packed dark brown sugar
½ teaspoon salt
¼ teaspoon black pepper
3 whole cloves

1. Melt butter in large skillet or large saucepan over medium heat. Add cabbage; cook and stir 3 minutes until cabbage is glossy. Transfer to 5-quart slow cooker.

2. Add apple, raisins, apple cider, 2 tablespoons vinegar, brown sugar, salt, pepper and cloves. Cover; cook on LOW 2½ to 3 hours.

3. Remove and discard cloves and stir in remaining 1 tablespoon vinegar.   *Makes 4 to 6 servings*

Prep Time: 15 minutes • **Cook Time:** 2½ to 3 hour

Rustic Potatoes au Gratin

½ cup milk
1 can (10¾ ounces) condensed Cheddar cheese soup, undiluted
1 package (8 ounces) cream cheese, softened
1 clove garlic, minced
¼ teaspoon ground nutmeg
⅛ teaspoon black pepper
2 pounds baking potatoes, cut into ¼-inch-thick slices
1 small onion, thinly sliced
Paprika (optional)

1. Heat milk in small saucepan over medium heat until small bubbles form around edge of pan. Remove from heat. Add soup, cream cheese, garlic, nutmeg and pepper. Stir until smooth.

2. Layer one fourth of potatoes and one fourth of onion in slow cooker. Top with one fourth of soup mixture. Repeat layers 3 times.

3. Cover; cook on LOW 6½ to 7 hours or until potatoes are tender and most liquid is absorbed. Sprinkle with paprika.

Makes 6 servings

Easy Holiday Stuffing

    1 cup butter, melted
    2 cups chopped celery
    1 cup chopped onion
    1 teaspoon poultry seasoning
    1 teaspoon leaf sage, crumbled
    ½ teaspoon ground black pepper
    3 tablespoons HERB-OX® chicken flavored bouillon
    2 eggs, beaten
    2 cups water
    12 cups dry breadcrumbs

In large bowl, combine butter, celery, onion, seasonings, bouillon, eggs and water together. Add breadcrumbs and stir to blend. Place mixture in 5-quart slow cooker. Cook on HIGH for 45 minutes; reduce heat to LOW and cook for 6 hours or cook on HIGH for 3 hours.

Makes 12 servings

Wild Rice and Dried Cherry Risotto

1 cup dry-roasted salted peanuts
2 tablespoons sesame oil, divided
1 cup chopped onion
4 cups hot water
6 ounces uncooked wild rice
1 cup diced carrots
1 cup chopped green or red bell pepper
½ cup dried cherries
⅛ to ¼ teaspoon red pepper flakes
¼ cup teriyaki or soy sauce
1 teaspoon salt, or to taste

1. Coat slow cooker with nonstick cooking spray. Heat large skillet over medium-high heat. Cook and stir peanuts 2 to 3 minutes or until beginning to brown. Transfer peanuts to plate.

2. Heat 2 teaspoons sesame oil in skillet. Cook and stir onions 6 minutes or until richly browned. Transfer to slow cooker.

3. Stir in water, wild rice, carrots, bell pepper, cherries and red pepper flakes. Cover; cook on HIGH 3 hours.

4. Let stand 15 minutes, uncovered, until liquid is absorbed. Stir in teriyaki sauce, peanuts, remaining sesame oil and salt.

Makes 8 to 10 servings

Prep Time: 5 minutes • **Cook Time:** 3 hours

Editor's Note

Wild rice is an underrated eating pleasure. Not only is it a nutritional powerhouse, but its nutty and earthy flavor is outstanding and adaptable.

Wild Rice and Dried Cherry Risotto

Donna's Potato Casserole

1 can (10¾ ounces) condensed cream of chicken soup, undiluted
1 cup (8 ounces) sour cream
¼ cup chopped onion
¼ cup (½ stick) plus 3 tablespoons butter, melted, divided
1 teaspoon salt
2 pounds potatoes, peeled and chopped
2 cups (8 ounces) shredded Cheddar cheese
1½ to 2 cups stuffing mix

1. Combine soup, sour cream, onion, ¼ cup butter and salt in small bowl.

2. Combine potatoes and cheese in slow cooker. Pour soup mixture over potato mixture; mix well. Sprinkle stuffing mix over potato mixture; drizzle with remaining 3 tablespoons butter.

3. Cover; cook on LOW 8 to 10 hours or on HIGH 5 to 6 hours until potatoes are tender. *Makes 8 to 10 servings*

Prep Time: 10 minutes • **Cook Time:** 8 to 10 hours (LOW) or 5 to 6 hours (HIGH)

Chunky Ranch Potatoes

3 pounds medium red potatoes, unpeeled and quartered
1 cup water
½ cup grated Parmesan or Cheddar cheese (optional)
½ cup prepared ranch dressing
¼ cup minced chives

1. Place potatoes and water in slow cooker. Cover; cook on LOW 7 to 9 hours or HIGH 4 to 6 hours or until potatoes are tender

2. Stir in cheese, if desired, ranch dressing and chives. Use spoon to break potatoes into chunks. *Makes 8 servings*

Prep Time: 10 minutes • **Cook Time:** 7 to 9 hours (LOW) or 4 to 6 hours (HIGH)

Donna's Potato Casserole

Southwestern Corn and Beans

1 tablespoon olive oil

1 large onion, diced

1 or 2 jalapeño peppers,* chopped

1 clove garlic, minced

2 cans (about 15 ounces each) red kidney beans, rinsed and drained

1 bag (16 ounces) frozen corn, thawed

1 can (about 14 ounces) diced tomatoes

1 green bell pepper, cut into 1-inch pieces

2 teaspoons chili powder

¾ teaspoon salt

½ teaspoon ground cumin

½ teaspoon black pepper

   Sour cream or plain yogurt (optional)

   Sliced black olives (optional)

Jalapeño peppers can sting and irritate the skin, so wear rubber gloves when handling peppers and do not touch your eyes.

1. Heat oil in medium skillet over medium heat. Add onion, jalapeño and garlic; cook and stir 5 minutes. Transfer to slow cooker.

2. Add beans, corn, tomatoes, bell pepper, chili powder, salt, cumin and black pepper to slow cooker; mix well. Cover; cook on LOW 7 to 8 hours or on HIGH 2 to 3 hours.

3. Serve with sour cream and black olives.   *Makes 6 servings*

Serving Suggestion: For a party, spoon this colorful vegetarian dish into hollowed-out bell peppers or bread bowls.

Prep Time: 15 minutes • **Cook Time:** 7 to 8 hours (LOW) or 2 to 3 hours (HIGH)

Southwestern Corn and Beans

Sweet Endings

English Bread Pudding

16 slices day-old, firm-textured white bread (1 small loaf)
1¾ cups milk
1 package (8 ounces) mixed dried fruit, cut into small pieces
½ cup chopped nuts
1 medium apple, chopped
⅓ cup packed brown sugar
¼ cup (½ stick) butter, melted
1 egg, lightly beaten
1 teaspoon ground cinnamon
¼ teaspoon ground nutmeg
¼ teaspoon ground cloves

1. Tear bread into 1- to 2-inch pieces; place in slow cooker. Pour milk over bread; let soak 30 minutes. Stir in dried fruit, nuts and apple.

2. Combine remaining ingredients in small bowl; pour over bread mixture. Stir well to blend. Cover; cook on LOW 3½ to 4 hours or until toothpick inserted into center of pudding comes out clean.

Makes 6 to 8 servings

Note: Chopping dried fruits can be difficult. To make the job easier, cut the fruit with kitchen scissors. Spray the scissors with nonstick cooking spray before chopping to prevent sticking.

Mulled Apple Cider

    2 quarts bottled apple cider or juice (not unfiltered)
   ¼ cup packed light brown sugar
    8 whole allspice
    4 cinnamon sticks, broken into halves
   12 whole cloves
    1 large orange
      Additional cinnamon sticks (optional)

1. Combine apple cider and brown sugar in 2½- to 3-quart slow cooker. Rinse 8-inch square cheesecloth; squeeze out water. Wrap allspice berries and cinnamon stick halves in cheesecloth; tie securely with cotton string or strip of cheesecloth. Cut orange into quarters; stick cloves randomly into orange peel. Place spice bag and orange quarters into slow cooker.

2. Cover; cook on HIGH 2½ to 3 hours.

3. Remove and discard spice bag and orange before serving. Garnish each serving with additional cinnamon sticks, if desired.

Makes 10 servings

Kitchen Tip

To make inserting cloves into the orange a little easier, first pierce the orange skin with the point of wooden skewer. Remove the skewer and insert a clove.

Mulled Apple Cider

Spiked Sponge Cake

Cake

> 1 package (about 18 ounces) yellow cake mix
> 1 cup water
> ½ cup vegetable oil
> 4 large eggs
> 1 tablespoon grated orange peel
> 1 package (6 ounces) golden raisins or dried cherries
> (about 1 cup)

Sauce

> 1 cup chopped pecans
> ½ cup sugar
> ½ cup (1 stick) butter, melted
> ¼ cup bourbon or apple juice

1. Generously coat 5-quart slow cooker with nonstick cooking spray. Cut parchment paper to fit bottom of stoneware and press into place. Spray paper lightly with nonstick cooking spray.

2. Combine cake mix, water, oil, and eggs in large bowl; stir well. Stir in orange peel. Pour two thirds of batter into slow cooker. Sprinkle dried fruits evenly over batter. Spoon on remaining batter evenly. Cover; cook on HIGH 1½ to 1¾ hours or until toothpick inserted into center of cake comes out clean.

3. Immediately remove stoneware from cooking base; cool 10 minutes on wire rack. Run flat rubber spatula around outer edges, lifting up bottom slightly. Invert onto serving plate. Peel off paper.

4. Heat large skillet over medium-high heat. Add pecans. Cook and stir 2 to 3 minutes or until pecans begin to brown. Add sugar, butter and bourbon and bring to a boil, stirring constantly. Cook 1 to 2 minutes longer or until sugar has dissolved. Pour sauce over entire cake or spoon sauce over each serving.   *Makes 8 to 10 servings*

Prep Time: 10 minutes • **Cook Time:** 1½ to 1¾ hours

Spiked Sponge Cake

Coconut Rice Pudding

2 cups water
1 cup uncooked converted long-grain rice
1 tablespoon unsalted butter
  Pinch salt
2¼ cups evaporated milk
  1 can (14 ounces) cream of coconut
  ½ cup golden raisins
  3 egg yolks, beaten
    Grated peel of 2 limes
  1 teaspoon vanilla
    Toasted shredded coconut (optional)

1. Coat slow cooker with nonstick cooking spray. Place water, rice, butter and salt in medium saucepan. Bring to a boil over high heat, stirring frequently. Reduce heat to low. Cover; cook 10 to 12 minutes. Pour rice mixture into slow cooker.

2. Add evaporated milk, cream of coconut, raisins, egg yolks, lime peel and vanilla into slow cooker; mix well. Add rice; stir until blended. Pour into prepared slow cooker.

3. Cover; cook on LOW 4 hours or on HIGH 2 hours. Stir once or twice during cooking. Pudding will thicken as it cools. Garnish with toasted shredded coconut.   *Makes 6 servings*

Prep Time: 20 minutes • **Cook Time:** 4 hours (LOW) or 2 hours (HIGH)

Editor's Note

Rice pudding is a diner classic that everyone loves. This version has the creamy sweet flavor of coconut and the tang from the lime peel. It's a dessert not to be missed.

Coconut Rice Pudding

Mocha Supreme

2 quarts strong brewed coffee
½ cup instant hot chocolate beverage mix
1 cinnamon stick, broken into halves
1 cup whipping cream
1 tablespoon powdered sugar

1. Combine coffee and hot chocolate mix in 3- to 3½-quart slow cooker; stir until well blended. Add cinnamon sticks. Cover; cook on HIGH 2 to 2½ hours.

2. Remove and discard cinnamon sticks. Beat cream in medium bowl with electric mixer at high speed until soft peaks form. Add powdered sugar; beat until stiff peaks form. Ladle hot beverage into mugs; top with whipped cream.

Makes 8 servings

Note: You can whip cream faster if you first chill the beaters and bowls in the freezer for 15 minutes.

Pineapple Daiquiri Sundae Topping

1 pineapple, peeled, cored and cut into ½-inch chunks
½ cup dark rum
½ cup sugar
  Peel of 2 limes, cut into long strips
3 tablespoons lime juice
1 tablespoon cornstarch
  Ice cream, pound cake or shortcake
  Fresh raspberries and mint leaves (optional)

Place pineapple, rum, sugar, lime peel, lime juice and cornstarch in 1½-quart slow cooker; mix well. Cover; cook on HIGH 3 to 4 hours. Serve hot over ice cream, pound cake or shortcakes. Garnish with raspberries and mint leaves.

Makes 4 to 6 servings

Variation: Substitute 1 can (20 ounces) crushed pineapple, drained, for the fresh pineapple. Cook on HIGH 3 hours.

Prep Time: 10 minutes • **Cook Time:** 3 to 4 hours

Mocha Supreme

Spiced Plums and Pears

2 cans (29 ounces each) sliced pears in heavy syrup, undrained
2 pounds black or red plums (about 12 to 14), pitted and sliced
1 cup packed brown sugar
1 teaspoon ground cinnamon
½ teaspoon ground ginger
¼ teaspoon grated lemon peel
2 tablespoons cornstarch
2 tablespoons water
   Pound cake or ice cream
   Whipped topping

1. Cut pear slices in half with spoon. Place pears, plums, sugar, cinnamon, ginger and lemon peel in slow cooker. Cover; cook on HIGH 4 hours.

2. Combine cornstarch and water to make smooth paste. Stir into slow cooker. Cook on HIGH 15 minutes until slightly thickened.

3. Serve warm or at room temperature over pound cake with whipped topping.   *Makes 6 to 8 servings*

Note: Also, serve as a condiment with baked ham, roast pork or roast turkey.

Prep Time: 10 minutes • **Cook Time:** 4 hours

Peach Cobbler

2 packages (16 ounces each) frozen peaches, thawed and drained
¾ cup plus 1 tablespoon sugar, divided
2 teaspoons ground cinnamon, divided
½ teaspoon ground nutmeg
¾ cup all-purpose flour
6 tablespoons butter, cut into bits
   Whipped cream (optional)

1. Combine peaches, ¾ cup sugar, 1½ teaspoons cinnamon and nutmeg in medium bowl. Place into slow cooker.

2. Combine flour, remaining 1 tablespoon sugar and remaining ½ teaspoon cinnamon in small bowl. Cut in butter with pastry blender or 2 knives until mixture resembles coarse crumbs. Sprinkle over peach mixture. Cover; cook on HIGH 2 hours.

3. Serve with whipped cream, if desired.   *Makes 4 to 6 servings*

Triple Chocolate Pudding Cake with Raspberry Sauce

    Vegetable cooking spray
1 package (about 18 ounces) chocolate cake mix
1 package (about 3.9 ounces) chocolate instant pudding and
    pie filling mix
2 cups sour cream
4 eggs
1 cup V8® 100% Vegetable Juice
¾ cup vegetable oil
1 cup semi-sweet chocolate pieces
    Raspberry dessert topping
    Whipped cream

1. Spray the inside of a 4-quart slow cooker with the cooking spray.

2. Beat the cake mix, pudding mix, sour cream, eggs, vegetable juice and oil in a large bowl with an electric mixer on medium speed for 2 minutes. Stir in the chocolate pieces. Pour the batter into the cooker.

3. Cover and cook on LOW for 6 to 7 hours or until a knife inserted in the center comes out with moist crumbs. Serve with the raspberry topping and whipped cream.   *Makes 12 servings*

Kitchen Tip: Use your favorite chocolate cake mix and pudding mix flavor in this recipe: chocolate, devil's food, dark chocolate or chocolate fudge.

Prep Time: 10 minutes • **Cook Time:** 6 hours

Glazed Cinnamon Coffee Cake

Streusel

¼ cup biscuit baking mix

¼ cup packed light brown sugar

½ teaspoon ground cinnamon

Batter

1½ cups biscuit baking mix

¾ cup granulated sugar

½ cup vanilla or plain yogurt

1 large egg, lightly beaten

1 teaspoon vanilla

Glaze

1 to 2 tablespoons milk

1 cup powdered sugar

½ cup sliced almonds (optional)

1. Generously coat 4-quart slow cooker with nonstick cooking spray. Cut parchment paper to fit bottom of stoneware and press into place. Spray paper lightly with cooking spray.

2. Blend ¼ cup baking mix, brown sugar and cinnamon in small bowl.

3. Mix 1½ cups baking mix, granulated sugar, yogurt, egg and vanilla in medium bowl until well blended. Spoon half of batter into slow cooker. Sprinkle half of streusel over top. Repeat with remaining batter and streusel.

4. Line lid with 2 paper towels. Cover; cook on HIGH 1¾ to 2 hours or until toothpick inserted into center comes out clean and cake springs back when gently pressed. Allow cake to rest 10 minutes. Invert onto plate; peel off paper. Invert again onto serving plate.

5. Whisk milk into powdered sugar 1 tablespoon at a time until desired consistency. Spoon glaze over top of cake. Garnish with sliced almonds, if desired. Cut into wedges. *Makes 6 to 8 servings*

Prep Time: 10 minutes • **Cook Time:** 1¾ to 2 hours

Glazed Cinnamon Coffee Cake

Chocolate Almond Bread Pudding with Dried Cherries

Vegetable cooking spray
10 slices PEPPERIDGE FARM® White Sandwich Bread, cut into cubes (about 5 cups)
½ cup dried cherries, chopped
½ cup semi-sweet chocolate pieces
1¾ cups milk
½ cup sugar
⅓ cup unsweetened cocoa powder
½ teaspoon almond **or** vanilla extract
4 eggs, beaten
Sweetened whipped cream (optional)
Toasted almonds (optional)

1. Spray the inside of a 4½- to 5-quart slow cooker with the cooking spray.

2. Place the bread cubes into the cooker. Sprinkle with the cherries and chocolate.

3. Beat the milk, sugar, cocoa, vanilla and eggs in a medium bowl with a fork or whisk. Pour over the bread mixture. Stir and press the bread cubes into the milk mixture to coat.

4. Cover and cook on LOW for 2½ to 3 hours or until set. Serve warm with the whipped cream and almonds, if desired.

Makes 6 servings

Prep Time: 10 minutes • **Cook Time:** 2½ to 3 hours

Kitchen Tip

This recipe is also delicious with white chocolate chunks instead of the semi-sweet chocolate pieces.

Chocolate Almond Bread Pudding with Dried Cherries

Chai Tea

    2 quarts (8 cups) water
    8 tea bags black tea
    ¾ cup sugar*
   16 whole cloves
   16 whole cardamom seeds, pods removed (optional)
    5 cinnamon sticks
    8 slices fresh ginger
    1 cup milk

Chai tea is typically a sweet drink. For less sweet tea, reduce sugar to ½ cup.

1. Combine water, tea bags, sugar, cloves, cardamom, if desired, cinnamon sticks and ginger in slow cooker. Cover; cook on HIGH 2 to 2½ hours.

2. Strain mixture; discard solids. (At this point, tea may be covered and refrigerated up to 3 days). Stir in milk just before serving. Serve warm or chilled. *Makes 8 to 10 servings*

Prep Time: 8 minutes • **Cook Time:** 2 to 2½ hours

Poached Pears with Raspberry Sauce

    4 cups cran-raspberry juice cocktail
    2 cups Rhine or Riesling wine
    ¼ cup sugar
    2 cinnamon sticks, broken into halves
    4 to 5 firm Bosc or Anjou pears, peeled
    1 package (10 ounces) frozen raspberries in syrup, thawed
      Fresh berries (optional)

1. Combine juice, wine, sugar and cinnamon sticks in slow cooker. Submerge pears in mixture. Cover; cook on LOW 3½ to 4 hours or until pears are tender.

2. Remove and discard cinnamon sticks. Process raspberries in food processor or blender until smooth; strain and discard seeds. Spoon raspberry sauce onto serving plates; place pears on top of sauce. Garnish with fresh berries. *Makes 4 to 5 servings*

Chai Tea

Steamed Pumpkin Cake

1½ cups all-purpose flour
1½ teaspoons baking powder
1½ teaspoons baking soda
 1 teaspoon ground cinnamon
½ teaspoon salt
¼ teaspoon ground cloves
 2 cups packed light brown sugar
½ cup (1 stick) butter, melted
 3 eggs, beaten
 1 can (15 ounces) solid-pack pumpkin
   Sweetened whipped cream (optional)

1. Grease 2½-quart soufflé dish or casserole that fits into slow cooker.

2. Combine flour, baking powder, baking soda, cinnamon, salt and cloves in medium bowl.

3. Beat brown sugar, butter and eggs in large bowl with electric mixer at medium speed until creamy. Beat in pumpkin. Stir in flour mixture. Spoon batter into prepared dish.

4. Fill slow cooker with 1 inch hot water. Make foil handles, using technique described below, to allow for easy removal of soufflé dish. Cover; cook on HIGH 3 to 3½ hours or until toothpick inserted into center of cake comes out clean.

5. Use foil handles to lift dish from slow cooker. Cool on wire rack 15 minutes. Invert cake onto serving platter. Cut into wedges and serve with dollop of whipped cream. *Makes 12 servings*

Foil Handles: Tear off 3 (18×2-inch) strips of heavy foil, or use regular foil folded to double thickness. Crisscross foil strips in spoke design and place in slow cooker. Place dish in center; pull foil strips up and over dish.

Serving Suggestion: Enhance this cake with a topping of sautéed apples or pear slices, or perhaps even a scoop of pumpkin ice cream.

Prep Time: 15 minutes • **Cook Time:** 3 to 3½ hours

Steamed Pumpkin Cake

Acknowledgments

The publisher would like to thank the companies and organizations listed below for the use of their recipes and photographs in this publication.

Bob Evans®

Cabot® Creamery Cooperative

Campbell Soup Company

ConAgra Foods, Inc.

Hormel Foods, LLC

Reckitt Benckiser Inc.

Dips & Spreads *(continued)*
Chunky Pinto Bean Dip, 10
Shrimp Fondue Dip, 16
Spicy Apple Butter, 84
Donna's Potato Casserole, 116

E

Easy Beef Stew, 28
Easy Dirty Rice, 110
Easy Holiday Stuffing, 113
English Bread Pudding, 120

F

Fiesta Black Bean Soup, 28
French Toast Bread Pudding, 82

G

Glazed Cinnamon Coffee Cake, 132
Greek Chicken and Orzo, 78
Greek Chicken Pitas with Creamy Mustard Sauce, 69

H

Ham and Cheddar Brunch Strata, 94
Ham with Fruited Bourbon Sauce, 58
Hearty Beef & Bean Chili, 26
Hearty Pork Stew, 44

I

Italian Hillside Garden Soup, 34

J

Jambalaya, 38

L

Lamb
Lamb and Vegetable Stew, 42
Lamb Shank and Mushroom Stew, 35
Moroccan-Style Lamb Shoulder Chops with Couscous, 68
Lentil Soup with Beef, 36

M

Mahogany Wings, 13
Mini Swiss Steak Sandwiches, 22
Mocha Supreme, 128
Moroccan-Style Lamb Shoulder Chops with Couscous, 68
Mulled Apple Cider, 122
My Mother's Sausage & Vegetable Soup, 36

N

New Mexican Green Chile Pork Stew, 30
No-Fuss Macaroni & Cheese, 104
Noodles & Pasta
Creamy Beef Stroganoff, 48
Greek Chicken and Orzo, 78
Italian Hillside Garden Soup, 34
Lamb Shank and Mushroom Stew, 35
Moroccan-Style Lamb Shoulder Chops with Couscous, 68
No-Fuss Macaroni & Cheese, 104
Pasta Fagioli Soup, 24
Spinach and Ricotta Stuffed Shells, 74

O

Oatmeal Crème Brûlée, 86
Orange Cranberry-Nut Bread, 92
Orange Date-Nut Bread, 102
Orange-Spiced Sweet Potatoes, 106
Osso Bucco, 60

P

Pasta Fagioli Soup, 24
Peach Cobbler, 130
Pineapple
Chicken Teriyaki, 62
Pineapple Daiquiri Sundae Topping, 128
Slow Cooker Sweet and Sour Brats, 62
Poached Pears with Raspberry Sauce, 136
Polska Kielbasa with Beer & Onions, 76
Pork
Bacon and Cheese Brunch Potatoes, 88
Barbecued Franks, 18
Cheese Grits with Chiles and Bacon, 93
Chorizo Chili, 32
Coq au Vin, 57
Easy Dirty Rice, 110
Fiesta Black Bean Soup, 28
Ham and Cheddar Brunch Strata, 94
Ham with Fruited Bourbon Sauce, 58
Hearty Pork Stew, 44
Italian Hillside Garden Soup, 34
New Mexican Green Chile Pork Stew, 30
Polska Kielbasa with Beer & Onions, 76
Sausage and Swiss Chard Stuffed Mushrooms, 12

VOLUME MEASUREMENTS (dry)

$1/8$ teaspoon = 0.5 mL
$1/4$ teaspoon = 1 mL
$1/2$ teaspoon = 2 mL
$3/4$ teaspoon = 4 mL
1 teaspoon = 5 mL
1 tablespoon = 15 mL
2 tablespoons = 30 mL
$1/4$ cup = 60 mL
$1/3$ cup = 75 mL
$1/2$ cup = 125 mL
$2/3$ cup = 150 mL
$3/4$ cup = 175 mL
1 cup = 250 mL
2 cups = 1 pint = 500 mL
3 cups = 750 mL
4 cups = 1 quart = 1 L

VOLUME MEASUREMENTS (fluid)

1 fluid ounce (2 tablespoons) = 30 mL
4 fluid ounces ($1/2$ cup) = 125 mL
8 fluid ounces (1 cup) = 250 mL
12 fluid ounces ($1 1/2$ cups) = 375 mL
16 fluid ounces (2 cups) = 500 mL

WEIGHTS (mass)

$1/2$ ounce = 15 g
1 ounce = 30 g
3 ounces = 90 g
4 ounces = 120 g
8 ounces = 225 g
10 ounces = 285 g
12 ounces = 360 g
16 ounces = 1 pound = 450 g

DIMENSIONS

$1/16$ inch = 2 mm
$1/8$ inch = 3 mm
$1/4$ inch = 6 mm
$1/2$ inch = 1.5 cm
$3/4$ inch = 2 cm
1 inch = 2.5 cm

OVEN TEMPERATURES

250°F = 120°C
275°F = 140°C
300°F = 150°C
325°F = 160°C
350°F = 180°C
375°F = 190°C
400°F = 200°C
425°F = 220°C
450°F = 230°C

BAKING PAN SIZES

Utensil	Size in Inches/Quarts	Metric Volume	Size in Centimeters
Baking or Cake Pan (square or rectangular)	$8 \times 8 \times 2$	2 L	$20 \times 20 \times 5$
	$9 \times 9 \times 2$	2.5 L	$23 \times 23 \times 5$
	$12 \times 8 \times 2$	3 L	$30 \times 20 \times 5$
	$13 \times 9 \times 2$	3.5 L	$33 \times 23 \times 5$
Loaf Pan	$8 \times 4 \times 3$	1.5 L	$20 \times 10 \times 7$
	$9 \times 5 \times 3$	2 L	$23 \times 13 \times 7$
Round Layer Cake Pan	$8 \times 1 1/2$	1.2 L	20×4
	$9 \times 1 1/2$	1.5 L	23×4
Pie Plate	$8 \times 1 1/4$	750 mL	20×3
	$9 \times 1 1/4$	1 L	23×3
Baking Dish or Casserole	1 quart	1 L	—
	$1 1/2$ quart	1.5 L	—
	2 quart	2 L	—